# SALES GENIUS

# Sales Genius

A master class in successful selling

Tony Buzan and Richard Israel

Illustrations by Dru Fuller

Gower

Published by
Gower Publishing Limited
Gower House
Croft Road
Aldershot
Hampshire GU11 3HR
England

Gower
Old Post Road
Brookfield
Vermont 05036
USA


Tony Buzan and Richard Israel have asserted their right under the Copyright, Designs and Patents Act 1988 to be identified as the authors of this work.

Inner Modelling is the registered trademark of Inner Modelling Inc.
Conni Gordon Four-Step Method is the registered trademark of Conni Gordon.
Mind Maps® is the registered trademark of the Buzan Organisation.

British Library Cataloguing in Publication Data
Buzan, Tony
  Sales genius : a master class in successful selling
  1. Selling 2. Sales promotion 3. Selling – Psychological
  aspects
  I. Title II. Israel, Richard, 1942–
  658.8'5


ISBN 0 566 08209 8 Paperback


Library of Congress Cataloging-in-Publication Data
Buzan, Tony.
    Sales genius : a master class in successful selling / Tony Buzan
  and Richard Israel : Illustrations by Dru Fuller.
      p.   cm.
    Includes index.
    ISBN 0–566–08209–8 (pbk.)
      1. Selling. I. Israel, Richard, 1942–. II. Fuller, Dru.
  III. Title.
  HF5438.25.B894   1999
  658.85—dc 21
                                                              99–11289
                                                              CIP


Typeset in Palatino by Bournemouth Colour Press, Parkstone and printed in Great Britain by MPG Books Ltd, Bodmin.

# Contents

## 12 Sales Intelligences Activities

# List of figures

# Preface

It was only a few short years ago that we published our first sales book on whole-brain selling – *Brain Sell*. Up to then sales books by the thousands had been written with emphasis on developing the selling skills of the brain's left cortical skills! Convinced that only half the story had been told, we wrote *Brain Sell* explaining how to use the *whole creative brain* in the sales process. We waited for the market's response to this revolutionary approach to selling. Our question was 'Was *Brain Sell* a book whose time had come?' Within a few months foreign rights to *Brain Sell* were being snapped up! It is now published in Chinese, Danish, Dutch, French, German, Hebrew, Polish, Romanian, Spanish and Turkish – and in two English versions, the United Kingdom and the United States of America. More translations are to follow! *SuperSelf* was placed in a cartoon strip, to enable easy access to the key points.

Needless to say, research on the human brain continues at an unrelenting pace. Soon we had new and exciting materials for a sequel.

At last we are able to dispel the myth that salespeople are born not made. In the pages that follow you will discover how easy it is to become a Sales Genius!

We owe special mention to the following: Ralph Roberts, a sales genius; Vanda North, our in-house editor and cheerleader extraordinary; Gwen Carden for her insights and editorial expertise; Conni Gordon, our friend and inspiration; Dru Fuller for her excellent artwork; Terry Brock for advice on technical intelligence; Nancy Rosanoff for her mastery on the intuition material; Eric Pillinger and the TACK team for initially marketing our Brain Sell and Master Class sales workshops; the Buzan Centres worldwide and all the Radiant instructors for carrying the flag; Tony and Michel Dottino, our dear friends and leading edge thinkers; Cliff Shaffran and the Quicksilver Group who are creating a new industry in thinking, learning and communicating; Helen Whitten, a brain star in the making; Dilip Mukerjea who continues to creatively amaze us; Malcolm Stern and the gang at Gower who continue to believe in our vision of a Mentally Literate world. To all of them, 'Thank you'.

Tony Buzan
Richard Israel

Tony Buzan
c/o The Buzan Centres Ltd
54 Parkstone Road
Poole
Dorset BH15 2PG
England
Tel: 44 (0) 1202 674676
Fax: 44 (0) 1202 674776
E-mail: Buzan@Mind-Map.com
Website: www.Mind-Map.com

Richard Israel
900 NE 195th Street, Suite 606
Miami
FL 33179
USA

Tel: 1 (305) 655-2675
Fax: 1 (305) 770-0926
E-mail: Brainsell@aol.com
Website: www.qsilvertlc.com

# How to use this book

## The purpose of the book

To show you how you can easily become a Sales Genius, even if you now think you could never be good at sales.

It doesn't matter if you aren't working in the sales profession. You are selling yourself all the time – selling ideas at work, selling the children the idea of behaving in a responsible way, selling yourself to the bank manager to obtain a loan, selling your partner on the restaurant or movie of your choice. Everyone is selling – even doctors, lawyers and accountants. In the new global economy, competition is ferocious and those who can't sell themselves sell themselves short!

Believe it or not, anyone who applies the principles in this book is only 100 days away from becoming a Sales Genius. You are a diamond in the rough. We'll show you how to cut and polish that diamond so that it becomes worth more than you ever imagined.

## How the book is organized

Much thought has been given to how to make this material as easy as possible for you to both understand and utilize the secrets of the Sales Genius formula.

Simplicity is the ultimate form of sophistication. (Leonardo da Vinci)

The book is divided into three Parts. Part One concentrates on what it takes to be a successful salesperson. First, we introduce you to an actual Sales Genius in the form of Ralph Roberts who displays our 12 traits of a Sales Genius:

1   having a peak sales vision
2   planning
3   persistence
4   learning from mistakes
5   belief in self, company, product and/or service
6   expertise
7   commitment
8   having a desire to succeed
9   having a mastermind group
10  truth and honesty
11  imagination
12  energy.

You will then learn about the most recent research into both your own brain and the 'customer's' brain – and how to take this new information and turn it into more successful 'selling'.

In recent years it's become apparent that intelligence is far more wide-ranging than being skilful in traditional academic subjects such as maths, science and English. In *Sales Genius* we focus on 12 elements of 'intelligence': verbal skills, logic, spatial awareness, senses, visualization skills, mind–body coordination, creativeness, people skills, personal management, musical, intuitiveness and technical aptitudes.

We have included a 60-question questionnaire to help you ascertain which of the above elements prevail and which are lying dormant. With this knowledge you will be able to select activities from Part Three which will maintain your strong qualities and enhance those you haven't been fully using. With all 12 of your intelligences working at their maximum, you will enjoy a synergistic effect on both your work and personal life.

In Part Two we show you what makes potential customers buy. We explain the *pain* and *pleasure* motivators as well as the 'complete picture' method of selling with detailed instructions on how to develop unique sales presentations.

Finally, in Part Three, there is the Sales Genius Diary. Here we take the 12 traits of a Sales Genius and help you incorporate them into your repertoire of behaviour. We have broken them down into three groups of four. Each four will be practised for 33 days – the time it takes to acquire a new behaviour pattern. At the end of 100 days all 12 will be a part of your business and personal life. To help you monitor your progress we have included a self-scoring sheet which you are asked to complete at intervals. This feedback will help you benchmark your progress.

The 100-day diary gives you the opportunity to practise every aspect of the Sales Genius formula. Each page is designed to help you learn and apply new skills guaranteed to build rapidly your genius potential.

## The activities

We have spent years researching, refining and creating the most powerful exercises (which we term activities) and format possible to help you realize your full potential. However, for these activities to empower you to change your life you must faithfully carry them out. This means completing your journal entries every day and doing the daily activity. Just glancing over them and skimming through won't work.

It's important to make the commitment now to complete this programme. Like a marathon runner, to reach your goal of being a Sales Genius you need to do your daily exercise. There are no short-cuts. Should you miss a day, pick up where you left off as each activity is designed to develop a specific part of your sales intelligence and you need time to practise and master them all.

Regard the complete text as a workbook, not just the journal pages in Part Three. As you read, you will have new ideas – jot them down. Underline key words and concepts. This will all help in reviewing the book and retaining the material in your long-term memory.

# PART ONE

## What makes a Sales Genius?

# 1    Portrait of a Sales Genius

If you've bought this book, you probably want to become a Sales Genius but are uncertain that you have what it takes. The story below illustrates that when you apply the 12 traits of a Sales Genius described in Chapter 2, extraordinary things can happen to ordinary people.

## The Ralph Roberts story

Ralph Roberts wasn't born being the best at what he does. In fact, you'll read that he was pretty hopeless at other businesses. The key was that he found something he had a passion for, turned it into a dream and didn't mind working harder than anyone else he knew. We think you'll find his story fascinating and inspirational.

Ralph Roberts sells more houses than any real estate agent in America – so many, in fact, that in 1995 *Time* magazine named him 'America's top realtor' and described him as the country's 'scariest salesman'. Ralph manages to sell over 600 homes a year – more than two homes per weekday – and still has time left over for his family, his hobbies and his dreams. (The average real estate agent sells 11 homes a year.) For nine years out of the past 11, he's been named the number one residential real estate agent in North America out of over 1 million agents, being placed second the other two years. Ralph is so good that real estate agents from around the country pay for the opportunity to 'shadow' him so they can learn about the methods he uses.

After spending just one day with Ralph, one agent, Sam Miller from Mt Vernon, Ohio, nearly tripled his productivity, increasing his sales from his already high 50 to more than 140 homes a year. By anyone's standards, Ralph is a Sales Genius.

Born in 1956, he got a job as a teenager cutting a neighbour's lawn for $10 a time, when all the neighbourhood kids were charging $5 – because he convinced the neighbour he'd do a better job. As a recent high school graduate in 1975, the Warren, Michigan dynamo took $900 and invested it in a three-bedroom house. 'I moved in and rented out all three bedrooms to different people,' said Ralph, author of *Walk Like A Giant, Sell Like A Madman*. 'I lived in the hallway.'

Over the next 15 years, Ralph lived in 23 homes, selling each one at a profit and moving on to the next opportunity. He didn't even let his wedding slow him down. He had a buyer attend his reception where they signed papers as the guests and his understanding and supportive bride listened to the music and drank champagne! When the couple took a long overdue holiday cruise he ran up a $1200 bill on the satellite phone system, making deals between bouts of seasickness.

To say that Ralph has a passion for his work is an understatement. He loves what he does, believes he is helping people and uses his success to help others by giving his money and his time to many local charitable organizations. Although Ralph seems to have been born with a knack for selling, he wasn't born knowing how to succeed. He claims that he was the class clown at school and could have been voted the 'most likely not to succeed'. In fact, he failed at several business ventures before discovering his gift of selling real estate. Setbacks in those other businesses discouraged him and he gave up, but he never gave up when he had setbacks in real estate. This was where his passion lay and, once he acknowledged that, and concentrated his efforts solely on real estate, there was no obstacle large enough to stop him. Despite the heartache they caused, Ralph says he's grateful for the failures which preceded his success because each one taught him valuable lessons that brought him closer to realizing his dreams.

'To be successful you must surround yourself with successful people,' says Ralph, who runs his real estate sales business with the help of a secretary, two listing agents, two buying agents and one closing coordinator. Of course, he didn't always understand that. By 1985 Ralph was already experiencing reasonable success and never bothered to attend professional meetings: 'I didn't think I could learn from anybody,' he confesses. But there was a national realtor convention in San Francisco, a city Ralph wanted to visit, so he attended it, with no intention of attending any meetings, so that he could write off the cost of the trip against his tax liabilities. Out of curiosity he decided to go to one or two of the sessions and was astounded to discover that, knowledgeable as he was, there was still much to learn and a great deal he could benefit from. Ralph learned that, to be the best in your field, continuing education was a must. Even though Ralph often gives classes, he also takes them, some more than once because 'there are different instructors each time and there's always something of value you can pick up that you didn't know before'.

Ralph believes that setting goals, writing them down with specifics about how you want to achieve them and visualizing them are absolutely essential for success. One of his goals is to pay $1 million a year in taxes. Another is to do $1 million a month in business with a particular investor group he works with. To symbolize this goal he often passes out fake $1 million notes to those investors. We don't think he has yet sent a fake $1 million note to the Inland Revenue Service, however.

His family has a personal goal book at home, each of his children has a goal book and he keeps one at his office, which he refers to daily. He has set one-, five-, ten-, fifteen-year and lifetime goals. 'If we see something in a magazine like a log cabin or some property on a lake that we like, we cut out the picture and put it with our goal list,' he explains. It's important to revise goals from time to time, he says, because your situation changes. He cautions about failing to do so. In 1988, one of the goals shared by Ralph and his wife was to have another child. They adopted one and considered their family complete. No one bothered to take that goal off the list, and Ralph's wife found herself pregnant with their third child three months later!

Twice a year, Ralph's key staff come to his house for a work day during which they storyboard the area in which they work. They set goals, brainstorm and put good ideas down in an 'idea of the week' book. Employees are encouraged to write ideas in the book whenever they occur, even if the timing isn't quite right yet for implementation. Ralph and his department heads look through this book regularly. Often they find a good idea they had forgotten about and realize that now is the time to implement it.

The book is also used to 'educate' new employees. 'When we hire someone we have them read the book and buy into the concept,' Ralph notes. 'If they don't, we don't want them working for us because we only want people with us who share our vision.'

To accomplish as much as Ralph does – he owns 15 real estate-related companies and has 72 employees – requires an extraordinary degree of time management. Ralph's system is so remarkable that he sometimes finds himself walking around his office at two or three in the afternoon with everything done for the day! 'Time is money and I figure that my time is worth about \$2000 an hour, so I do a lot of delegating and use technology quite a bit,' he explains. His philosophy? 'Do it, delegate it or ditch it.' Here are a few of his time-saving tricks:

- Ralph has dictaphones hooked up to his two telephones in the office, carries one around with him and has one on his bedside table. As he concludes a conversation with someone (or as he leaves a voice mail message for someone), he flips on the dictaphone, reviews all the specifics of what he has agreed to do – where and when a meeting will take place, with whom, what is to be achieved – then gives the tape to his secretary who enters all the information where it is needed, including in a client file Ralph keeps near his desk for quick referral (he also notes it in his planner). When ideas occur to him, he uses the dictaphones to note them down so they aren't forgotten.
- Ralph never attends meetings for sales or listings without bringing along other essential people such as a buyer's agent, mortgage broker or title agent (all from his own subsidiary companies). That way, paperwork that is normally sent out and might take days or weeks to complete is taken care of in an hour.
- To communicate with key people Ralph dictates his thoughts into his dictaphone. These are transcribed and distributed daily to them as memos, eliminating the need for time-consuming meetings.
- Ralph's managers are asked not to come to Ralph with problems without first filling out a problem resolution sheet. On it they write the problem and two possible solutions, choosing which of the two solutions seems better to them.

  'Ironically, I hardly ever see these sheets,' notes Ralph, 'because by the time the managers have written everything down, the solution is obvious and they handle it without my help. And when I do see the sheets, 90 per cent of the time they've put forward the right solution.'
- Ralph uses staff meetings to kill two birds with one stone. When he holds his weekly '52 Weeks to Success' training meetings for managers and salespeople, Ralph often brings in outside experts. He taperecords the sessions and has them transcribed so that they can be used as material for his next book.

Although Ralph is a Sales Genius, he's not infallible, so he encourages his key people to give him feedback. 'They have to be able to tell you the truth for your success to be longlasting,' he explains. 'You can't hire people to give you advice and then ignore it.' He admits that some of the feedback occasionally wounds his ego and that his initial response is often 'I can't believe I said that!', but after the initial sting he considers what has been said and makes changes if he feels they're justified.

One such situation involved changing Ralph's strict policy that business attire should be worn at all times. One of his managers suggested establishing a casual day to help office morale. Ralph finally gave in after agreeing a dress code he was comfortable with, and everybody was happy.

Persistence is a trait that came naturally to Ralph after he found his passion, because when you have passion the persistence is easy. When he's told 'no', Ralph considers it a 'know', meaning that the other person simply doesn't yet know enough to say 'yes'. A few years ago he lost a listing because another agent told a homeowner that they could get $129 000 for their home. Ralph maintained that it would only sell for $121 000 and told them he had a buyer at that price. 'After their dog ate half of my Hartman briefcase, they threw me out of their home very professionally,' Ralph recalls. Ralph didn't call them again but every month he sent them mailshots. Four months later, they called him! The house hadn't sold and they remembered him because of his visit as well as his mailings. Once again Ralph told them the truth – the market had now turned and the house would only sell for between $109 000 and $111 000. This time they believed him and Ralph sold the house for $112 500.

Being truthful has helped Ralph's business succeed, he says. 'There's no shame in making an honest error in judgement, but dishonesty will hurt you in the long run. The only way to be successful is to tell it to people like it really is: here's the problem and here's the solution, and only suggest solutions that are in their best interests. Sometimes their best interest means you make less money or none at all, but the referrals you will get from people who know you treated them that way will more than make up for what you lost.'

One way in which Ralph can make sure he is always straight with people is by setting himself high standards in terms of being an expert: 'I make sure that I know more than anyone else. This starts by surrounding myself with knowledgeable people, going to professional meetings and reading all the time.' Ralph scans newspapers and magazines for articles of interest, highlights the salient points, rips them out and reads or rereads them later. He considers himself to be a 'speed scanner'. Recently, before being interviewed about foreclosure – a topic he knows extremely well – he nevertheless had an assistant research the subject for the very latest information. Being less than the very best simply won't do in Ralph's book!

Another source of information for Ralph is his advisory board, which, in this book, we call a 'mastermind group'. Four times a year he meets with six friends and acquaintances from different lines of work. He tells them what he has done and what he plans to do and they give him feedback. One valuable outcome was persuading Ralph to put a monetary value on his time so he could use it more wisely. Another was the problem resolution sheet mentioned earlier. He also gets together twice a year with a group of agents who all make $1 million a year or more in commissions to discuss the same sort of topics.

Paying attention to details is important to Ralph's success. He keeps fake cellular phones with him to hand out to prospects' children because 'If you can win over the kids, the parents are a breeze.' He also instructs his employees never to park in a client's driveway. 'If someone has to leave, you have to stop what you are doing and start all over,' he says. 'You don't know what the people inside are saying to each other while you are out moving the car. This means you lose control. The only way to win is to get and keep self-control.'

Keeping a positive attitude is another key to Ralph's success. 'I put a positive spin on every situation, no matter how bleak,' he says. 'I may have ten failures a day, but I know I'm going to have 20 successes. It's a lot like Babe Ruth. Most people know that he hit more home runs than any other baseball player, but few people know that he also struck out more than anybody else.' Recently Ralph lost a key employee unexpectedly and was so devastated he almost considered cancelling his appointments for the day, but when someone asked him how he felt about the situation he replied, 'Well, at least now our building will be smoke free.' This employee was the only one in the company who smoked.

With so much going on in Ralph's life, one might wonder when he has time to do any creative thinking. He says he does it all the time. Inspiration comes out of the blue for him, often when he's relaxed. Sometimes when he's shaving he has a brilliant idea and scribbles it on the mirror in soap. Significant ideas and solutions sometimes come to him in his sleep. He wakes up, puts the idea on his dictaphone or calls the voice mail of an affected person, then goes back to sleep.

When he's relaxing at a movie, watching TV with his wife or playing with his train set ideas just appear. He says his creativity works overtime. He can't look at a tree without trying to figure out how to paint it, climb it or help it become taller, stronger and more beautiful.

Because he only sleeps three to four hours a night Ralph has mastered 'power-napping'. He closes his eyes for 15–20 minutes, visualizing whatever situation he's involved in, and his brain works on problems and ideas, such as going to high school football games and throwing his business cards up in the air the first time the crowd jumps out of their seats. 'I don't have brainstorming days, I have a brainstorming life,' he says.

# Summary

Ralph Roberts exhibits all the 12 traits of a Sales Genius described in Chapter 2 as well as many of the sales intelligences dealt with in Chapter 4.

Now that you know what can happen when you put Sales Genius traits to work for you, finish reading this book and then set to work building your own dreams just like Ralph Roberts.

# 2 The 12 traits of a Sales Genius

This chapter deals with the 12 traits that we have identified that make up a Sales Genius. As you read each of the definitions, consider how you are applying these traits to your sales career. Be as truthful with yourself as possible so that you can establish a benchmark before starting the 100-day programme for unleashing your Sales Genius.

## The traits

### 1 A Sales Genius has a peak sales vision

The brain is a success-driven mechanism and will continually strive to reach whatever goals you set. You may have often heard how important it is to set goals but, strangely enough, only 10 per cent of salespeople have a written sales goal!

Without a sales goal and/or sales vision, your brain has nothing to aim for, so it selects anything or anybody that comes along each day as its focus. The brain fills in its own activity for the day, and this goal may be unproductive – something like 'Hey, let's take the day off!' You may well find that days, weeks, months or even years go by without achieving anything, simply because you were not aware of the importance of setting a sales goal or sales vision.

Think of using this brain principle as being similar to having a bow and arrow which needs a target. The brain needs that target to aim at as it releases the arrow through the air. Without a target the arrow would land at random and would miss the strategic bull's eye! So it is with your brain. Either you have a strategic sales vision or a haphazard 'let's see what happens' outlook. Which approach do you think will bring you more success?

The term 'peak sales vision' is used to illustrate what you could expect to reach in sales within the next 12 months if you stretched yourself. It should be a target with an increase of 20–30 per cent on your last year's performance. You need to stretch yourself because if you don't, you will probably not grow and instil confidence in others.

As you will discover in Chapter 3, for maximum impact, the brain stores pictures and images in its long-term memory. We use a vision or picture of a goal as opposed to writing it down. Using words and numbers are two of the mental skills covered. If you construct your peak sales vision to incorporate as many of the mental skills as possible – words, numbers, pictures, colours and imagination – you will create and strengthen the mental picture you need to store in long-term memory. On the opposite page, which you may wish to photocopy, make a colour drawing of your peak sales vision, using your imagination and writing the words, numbers and images you feel are necessary to depict exactly what it is. For example, if you want to earn £100 000 in sales over the next 12 months, draw a picture of a person standing on top of a mountain holding a flag with £100 000 on the flag to symbolize your sales. This would be the image you would hold in your mind.

It is even more important to place this peak sales vision in a position where you can see it daily. This will encourage you to constantly think about it and work out creative strategies to achieve it, reinforcing the target your brain is aiming for.

## 2    A Sales Genius plans

One of our most important resources is time. How we use it largely determines the degree of our success. This limited resource needs careful planning. We know only too well in selling that there are not enough hours in a day to contact every prospect we would like to contact, to do paperwork and to get where we need to go.

Time is such a valuable resource that you should take as much care with it as you do your money. Every day, when you wake up, say, 'I have 24 hours ahead of me. How should they be spent?' Don't leave out important considerations that put balance in your life, such as time with your family,

Peak Sales Vision

We suggest that you make a photocopy of page 13, rather than deface your book by removing the page. Alternatively you could use an A4 sheet of paper, which is more easily transportable and could be pinned to your office wall.

relaxation, exercise, adequate sleep, general maintenance like personal shopping and telephone calls or meditation – but don't let those overshadow your work goals. You may need chunks of time to write sales proposals, study competitors' activities and read up on new products. All should be taken into consideration in planning your next day or week or month.

Relying on memory to plan and execute your time can be perilous to your financial health and sales career. Implementing some sort of time management system is imperative. This system can be as simple as an inexpensive diary or as sophisticated as a complex software program.

As well as time management you need some type of personal filing system to deal with the information overload that plagues us all daily. Can you find vital pieces of information when you need them? Is your desk tidy and well organized, uncluttered by little slips of paper? Can you easily access client information and notes about meetings? Do you have a foolproof follow-up system so you don't miss appointments? This is an integral part of time management because, without an organized system, you will waste countless hours looking for important information.

## 3   A Sales Genius is persistent

If you consider skills you have learned in the past, such as when you first learned to walk, talk or ride a bicycle, you may recall that the learning curve was bumpy – that is, you often fell over while learning to walk, slurred your words when learning to talk and often fell off the bicycle before perfecting your balance. However, with persistence you mastered all three of these skills. Unfortunately, we tend to forget these valuable lessons. In our hectic lives where we expect instant results, disappointments and setbacks can often cause us to give up.

A study of geniuses shows that, despite tremendous hardships, lack of resources, health problems and mental disabilities, they persisted. One of the main success strategies of persistence was our first trait, the 'peak sales vision', for, as we know, because the brain is a success mechanism that keeps on trying to reach the desired formula, its persistence can be guaranteed provided it has a target. Once again this shows how important it is to have a sales vision and/or sales goals.

A sales career can be regarded as a marathon run that will occupy many years of your life, rather than a 100-yard dash. You therefore need to be fit both physically and mentally and have the end in mind as you set off. Persistence is the fuel that will carry you to the finishing line.

Consider Thomas Edison and how his invention of the electric light bulb permanently affected the world and improved the quality of life. After

Edison had tried over 5000 ways to produce light by means of electricity and was accused of being insane for refusing to give up, he replied that, since he was the only person who knew so many ways in which his experiments did *not* work, he must therefore be the one who was nearest to the truth.

## 4   A Sales Genius learns from mistakes

How often have we heard salespeople tell us that they have over ten years of sales experience, yet their results are dismal? What they are really saying is that they have been conducting business the same way for ten years but haven't learned from their mistakes! Learning from mistakes is one of the most powerful methods you have at your disposal to improve your sales career. With a little introspection and courage you can go back through your diaries and/or client contacts, review each one and ask: 'Why did I lose that sale? Why did I lose that account? Is there a pattern that I continually repeat? Are there situations that I constantly avoid? What can I learn about myself from my past work history that can help improve my future performance?'

Another way to learn from mistakes is to ask for feedback. This feedback can be provided by associates, managers, clients and former clients. You may even obtain valuable feedback from family members, friends and acquaintances at clubs, churches and associations. Negative feedback can be painful, but it should not be discouraging. Push your ego to the sidelines and be thankful, because feedback is there to help you improve. However, always consider the source before taking to heart any negative feedback. Is the person qualified to make a valid judgement? Do they have all the facts and see the whole picture? If the answer is 'no', feel free to disregard it or to approach someone who *is* qualified to make that sort of judgement and ask their opinion.

If you receive positive feedback, enjoy it and feel comfortable. Say 'thank you'. Don't negate it by minimizing it either out loud or internally. Positive feedback is vital food for your self-esteem as long as you keep it in perspective.

## 5   A Sales Genius believes in self, the company and the product or service

Believing in yourself is crucial to success, because if you don't believe in yourself how can you expect your prospect or client to? Your energy level, tone of voice, posture and choice of words all indicate how you feel about yourself.

Think of a charismatic person you know and ask yourself what makes them attractive to others. Chances are that they have an extremely high belief in themselves, and that belief is communicated through their words, body language and attitude. Belief in yourself can derive from those 40 000 thoughts we have each day. What is the quality of those thoughts? Do you need to change your internal soundtrack with positive affirmations such as 'I am enjoying success' and 'I believe in my ability to be successful and reach my goals'? Repeat these affirmations daily several times and also write them down and place them in a prominent position so that they remind you how important it is to change that inner dialogue.

It's also important to engage regularly in some sort of activity in which you excel, whether it be playing golf, putting together jigsaw puzzles, doing community work or mentoring a child. These are self-esteem boosters which then translate into other areas of your life. Evaluate your work. Do you have a passion for what you are doing? Do you really want to do it? If not, your situation can affect your belief in yourself. Perhaps you need to rethink what you are doing with your life because when you *do* identify your passion, it will be easy to believe in yourself. You will know you are where you should be.

We all have encountered people who obviously didn't believe in their company or product. We've bought something from a person who behaved as if he or she didn't care whether or not they had that job or had a customer. In fact, they may have acted almost as if you were a nuisance. How did that make you feel? Are you keen to go back for a second experience? These certainly aren't people destined for a stellar sales career.

Belief is a key ingredient in sales success because it inspires a passion that energizes you, drives you forward and, most importantly, keeps you interested in your pursuit. As we mentioned in Chapter 1, without interest the brain performs poorly, forgetting names and faces, prices and specifications, delivery dates and follow-up.

Lack of belief results in mediocre effort. How would you feel if you didn't believe in smoking, yet you worked for a tobacco company? How good a salesperson could you possibly be for them?

Here's where you need to be brutally honest and ask yourself what you believe about your company, their sales policies, their sales and marketing strategies, their treatment of customers, follow-up service, product range, price points, quality, reliability and so on. All these questions need answers because they influence how you behave in front of prospects. If you have a problem with some of these factors, you need to take action instead of letting it simmer. Your most drastic action could be to consider a job change.

## 6   A Sales Genius is an expert

Albert Einstein. Thomas Edison. Bill Gates. Marie Curie. What do all these people have in common? Besides being geniuses they are all noted for extraordinary expertise in their chosen fields. Whereas until recent years knowledge was the prized possession of a privileged few and very expensive to obtain, the information revolution has now levelled the playing field. Never before, in the history of mankind, has so much knowledge been made accessible to so many. Walk into any public library. Sit down at a computer. Access the World Wide Web and, at your fingertips, you have more information than you could handle in a lifetime. There's yet more information from television, magazines, radio and newsletters in your particular field. The opportunity that this offers in a selling career is largely untapped by the average salesperson. Approaching your prospect armed with expertise and knowledge about your product or service increases your ability to make the sale because it inspires confidence, adds value and answers the customer's questions.

Would you buy a car from a salesperson who doesn't know the car's mpg or horsepower or safety rating? Would you fly on an airline that offers low-price fares because the pilots are young and inexperienced? People pay for and respect expertise. This is an age when anyone with initiative can develop expertise. Irrespective of what you are selling, you can take one aspect of your product or service and become an expert within a few weeks or months. Soon you will be referred to as the one 'in the know'. You will be able to write newsletters, articles, make presentations at your trade association and may even be considered by the media as an interview source.

How do you become an expert? Once you have decided on your area of expertise, set a goal. Your mind will start to search for the information that you will need to collect and file. Visit your local library. Read all relevant magazine articles and books. Visit bookshops. Find out which authors are writing books about your subject and when they might be in the area making presentations. Read trade journals and attend meetings on your area of expertise. Write to experts asking them for additional information.

Spend four to five hours every month sifting through the information you have collected. Arrange it into a logical order. From this order you will start seeing new ideas emerge which you can capture. You can take this further by writing articles and giving talks to establish yourself as an expert.

## 7   A Sales Genius has commitment

Once you have established the peak sales vision, you must be committed to reaching it. The popular press often carries stories of celebrities announcing what they intend to do in respect of their commitment. One of the more colourful characters who did this was the boxer Cassius Clay (Muhammad Ali), who would announce the exact round in which he would knock out his opponent. He was almost always on target.

Probably the best description of commitment comes from Johann Wolfgang von Goethe (1749–1832), the man believed to have had the highest IQ and largest vocabulary in history:

> Until one is committed there is hesitancy, a chance to draw back. Always ineffectiveness concerning all acts of initiative and creation. There is one elementary proof – the ignorance of which kills countless ideas and splendid plans. This is, that the moment one definitely commits oneself, then Providence moves too. All sorts of things occur to help one, that would never otherwise have occurred. A whole stream of events issues from the decision, raising in one's favour all manner of unforeseen incidents and material assistance, which no man could have dreamed would have come his way. Whatever you can do or dream you can, begin it. Boldness has genius, power and magic in it, begin it now.

## 8   A Sales Genius has desire

Desire can be regarded as the passion or fire that keeps you on target. Think of the things in your life that you have really desired – a relationship, a home, a car, a holiday, a promotion. Next consider how strong was your desire for each of these. You will know from your own personal life history that the stronger your desire the greater your success in acquiring it.

How do we develop this desire to achieve our goal? First, you have to be doing something you want to do. Second, you have to believe that it will benefit you in some way, emotionally or monetarily. Don't fool yourself into thinking that certain goals which you say you want are ones that you truly desire. A good test is to ask yourself 'Do I want this so badly that the cost, consequences and inconveniences of pursuing or achieving this desire are inconsequential?' For example, imagine that you've just been offered the position of sales director at your company – something you have desired for a long time. However, the position is in Argentina which means that you have to learn Spanish, relocate your family and disrupt your current way of life. If you don't see these sacrifices as stumbling blocks, if none of these facts dampens your enthusiasm for this position, you can be sure what you have felt is true desire.

If you truly desire something you find yourself thinking about it 24 hours a day, researching it, talking about it and taking steps in the right direction to reach that goal, such as attending classes, looking for a new, more promising job or making strategies.

## 9   A Sales Genius has a mastermind group

If you don't already have a network of friends who act as a support or 'mastermind' group, you are depriving yourself of a powerful genius tool.

No matter how intelligent you are, incorporating the mental input of others on your journey to success is like quadrupling your brain power. Write down the names of your most trusted personal and business friends with whom you are comfortable discussing your current business activities. At least once a month make a point of raising areas of concern about your career about which you would find their input valuable.

Most people are delighted to give you their advice and opinions and will enthusiastically do so. Do not overlook this priceless opportunity to tap into your mastermind group's brain. You will be amazed at the good ideas, advice and feedback you receive. If you don't already have such a group, consider who you might include, drawing from business acquaintances, customers, managers, friends and relatives.

The key premise of this group should be your ability to be open and honest with these people and tell them your current situation without embarrassment.

Why is this group important? For the following reasons:

- You need fresh insights into your ideas, strategies and situations as they arise. What better than a group of advisers who already know you and your goals?
- Your mastermind group brings different areas of expertise to the situation. For example, the group might incorporate accountants, lawyers, architects, businesspeople, schoolteachers, ministers or personal friends who really care about you. Each person brings their own life and work experience to assist you on your journey.
- There will be times when you need encouragement or a sounding board, when you want to pick up the telephone and speak to a member of your group who can cheer you up or offer advice or solutions.

If you don't have a mastermind group, here's how to form one:

- **Step 1**: Think carefully about who you would like to have in your group.

- **Step 2**: Write down their names.
- **Step 3**: Contact them. Tell them of your intentions, who else is in your group and ask if they are willing to be part of your mastermind group.

Stay in regular telephone contact with members of your group. Speak to each member either personally or by telephone at least once a month. In your conversations briefly mention what's happening in your sales career. To benefit from this group you must be willing to ask each person's opinion, consider their advice and critiques and act on anything they suggest which you consider potentially helpful.

Keep the group updated on your progress. Once a year, it would be a pleasant gesture to send each member a small token of your appreciation.

## 10   A Sales Genius is truthful and honest

In our book *Brain Sell* we introduced the concept of the truth-seeking brain. The brain needs the truth in order to make the right decisions. How would you feel if you were trying to decide whether to buy something and the salesperson withheld some vital information which would affect your decision? The brain needs the truth in order to do the best it can both to be successful and to survive.

One of the principal problems experienced by the sales profession for many years was that, in their pursuit of making a sale, salespeople did not tell the truth. The consequences have been disillusionment on the part of buyers and a tarnished image for the whole sales profession.

Salespeople must realize that they are customers, too, and the golden rule of honesty applies to them as well as to those from whom they buy. Truth and honesty in advertising has been brought about by public demand and legislated by governments around the world.

By telling the truth you are enhancing your own self-esteem, because it fosters respect from others as well as for yourself. Anything less than the truth will dissipate your energy for positive creative thinking and selling because you will be too busy covering up and trying to remember your deceptions while simultaneously destroying your own self-esteem.

A reputation for being truthful and honest is like money in the bank. It promotes goodwill between you and your clients, who will recommend you to others. There's no more powerful way to obtain new business than through personal recommendations. People prefer to do business with someone they can trust. Companies have built wonderful sales strategies on this single premise. Marks and Spencer's returns policy is one such example. They take back anything – no questions asked.

## 11    A Sales Genius has imagination

Imagination is one of our mental skills – one of the most powerful mental skills we have as it encompasses daydreaming and our ability to create our future.

What could be more important to a salesperson than to create internal images, to see thoughts and visualize the outcome of plans and goals? Imagination is also one of the cornerstones of memory. The more it is used the better the memory performance will be. It was Albert Einstein who said, 'Imagination is more important than knowledge. For knowledge is limited whereas imagination embraces the entire world, stimulates progress, giving birth to evolution.'

Many salespeople have been brought up with the limited belief that hard work will bring success. It is the authors' contention that imagination is far more powerful than hard work. That is not to say that geniuses do not work hard, but combining hard work with imagination gives a synergistic effect to achieve a winning formula. What you can imagine or dream about, you can achieve.

All salespeople should spend time developing their imaginative powers. This can be done by taking some coloured pens and paper and drawing ideas as they come to mind. It's strongly recommended that this be done at the same time every day in order for the brain to become familiar with the activity. Putting the idea down in the form of a picture helps you capture and develop it. It also becomes a source of future reference to help keep you on-track. Also, you may well find that, within a day or two, you might go back and add to the picture as your brain gives you more input.

The best approach to this exercise is to think about the problem or sales situation you are facing before you go to sleep. Tell yourself that, on awakening, you will have the solution. How often have you noticed that answers to problems that were unsolvable one day pop into your head the next, while walking the dog, drinking coffee or reading the morning newspaper? These solutions come from your brain's ability to take the problem and, while you're sleeping or relaxing, integrate the information, sending it backwards and forwards through the left and right hemispheres and through the corpus callosum, creating imaginative solutions.

It would therefore be wonderful each morning, on awakening, to spend 5–10 minutes downloading all the imaginative work that your brain has done overnight. Unfortunately, due to the hurried lifestyle that we live, mornings are usually too hectic for many of us. Should this be the case, always have a pen and some paper at hand so that you can jot down ideas as soon as they arise.

Another technique for developing imaginative power is Tony Buzan's

Mind Mapping. A Mind Map is a powerful graphic technique, which provides a universal key to unlocking the potential of the brain. It harnesses the full range of cortical skills described in Chapter 3 – numbers, words, logic, lists, details, pictures, colour, imagination, rhythm and spatial awareness – in a single, uniquely powerful manner. In so doing, it gives you the freedom to roam the infinite expanses of your brain. The Mind Map can be applied to every aspect of business where improved learning and clearer thinking will improve your performance.

Like a road map, a Mind Map will:

- give you a quick, one-page overview of a large subject/area
- enable you to plan strategy/make choices
- let you know where you are going, and where you have been
- gather and hold large amounts of data on one page
- encourage both daydreaming and problem-solving by highlighting creative pathways
- allow you to be extremely efficient
- be enjoyable to look at, read, muse over and remember.

Figure 2.1 gives an example of a Mind Map, 'The Intelligence Revolution' by Pauline Wong and Wilson Ho, of Quicksilver Limited. Using a software program, MindManager, which is an example of a new level of integration of human and artificial intelligence, they have summarized a Hewlett Packard magazine article by Tony Buzan.

## 12   A Sales Genius is energetic

Without exception the great geniuses were known to exude an unusual degree of physical and mental energy. It's our contention that these expressions are natural and to be expected when a mind has a vision to which all other attributes of genius are attached. Unlike a factory which has machines to produce wealth, salespeople rely solely on their own daily activities to be productive. Energy is the vital ingredient that keeps the salesperson's engine running.

Successful salespeople have a positive mental attitude which energizes both their brains and their bodies. Energy can take various forms, both mental and physical. Mental energy requires looking after your brain by ensuring that it has adequate oxygen and fuel through diaphragmatic breathing, eating the right foods and having sufficient sleep. Physical energy comes from taking good care of our bodies, exercising, maintaining a positive mental attitude, refraining from excessive alcohol consumption and cutting out nicotine.

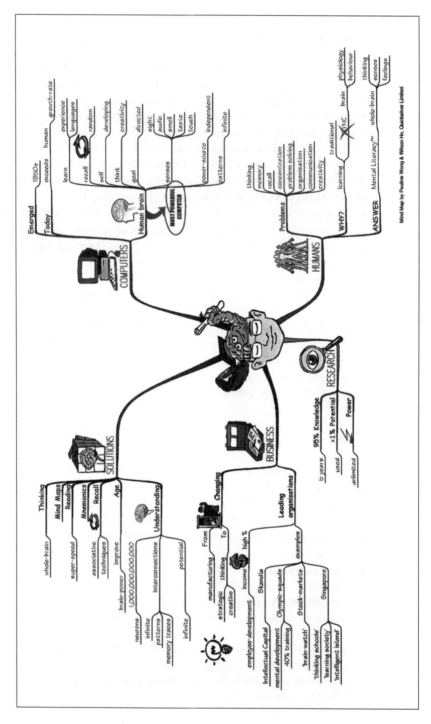

**Figure 2.1** The intelligence revolution

Energy comes from external sources as well. Achievements and the receiving of positive feedback provide outside, psychological sources of energy.

What gives you energy? When you get up on Monday morning to go to work, how energetic do you feel? Did you prefer staying up too late on Sunday night to retiring to bed early so you could start the week on the right foot? If you find that you are not energetic, an easy technique is to change your internal picture to make it more attractive and more compelling so that you feel energized when you look at it.

For example, when people think about an imminent holiday or party, their energy level rises. They become enthusiastic as they talk about it, think about it and plan for it. This is simply a consequence of a mental picture of some future event that they are holding in their mind. By changing the picture, you can change your energy level. It merely takes practice.

Power-napping is another way of regaining energy during the course of the day. A 10- to 20-minute power-nap can refresh you and extend your alertness for up to two hours after the time of night when you might normally become sleepy. Many geniuses are known to have practised this habit, one of the most famous being Winston Churchill. Power-naps lasting over an hour may have the opposite effect and make you drowsy. Not everyone can fall asleep quickly. It takes practice, a quiet uninterrupted space and the ability to relax and close down the mind.

# Summary

In this chapter we covered the 12 traits that make up the Sales Genius formula:

- peak sales vision
- planning
- persistence
- learning from mistakes
- belief in self, company, product/service
- expertise
- commitment
- desire
- mastermind group
- truth and honesty
- imagination
- energy.

The formula appears again in Part Three, 'The Sales Genius Diary'.

# 3    Your brain

## Your sleeping giant

Most of us know little about that sleeping giant we carry around with us all our lives called our brain. Why? Because the study of the brain is in its infancy! 95 per cent of what we know about the human brain has been discovered during the last five years.

The human brain has only existed in its present form for some 45 000 years – a mere twinkling of an eye in the context of evolutionary history – yet it has the capacity to store more data than all the libraries in the world. The total number of connections found in all the world's telephone systems would take up a space of less than the size of a pea in your brain. The number of thought patterns that your brain can make is greater than the number of atoms in the known universe, and to write them all out would require a piece of paper 10.5 million km in length. Just think what would happen to your sales career if you could harness a power of this magnitude!

If you buy a home computer you receive a bulky instruction manual, but where is the operational manual for your brain? Perhaps we can find some clues from the great brains of history. They used the breadth and depth of their intellectual skills – artistic as well as scientific abilities – all in a creative combination, to achieve outstanding results. They were able to think in many directions at once – what we term 'radiant thinking'. One of the principal ways in which your brain works is by associating, connecting and linking data, words, facts and all the senses in a fabulous intranetwork inside your head. The more these patterns are repeated, the more creative your brain becomes, especially when you incorporate the full range of your mental skills.

We have two upper brains. Research has shown that each one has a tendency to deal with a slightly different set of intellectual functions. Joining the two sections is an intricate bundle of nerves down the centre known as the corpus callosum. It is across the corpus callosum that the brain shuttles back and forth its amazing number of messages and data.

While the left hemisphere is creating words, the right hemisphere is creating a picture (see Figure 3.1).

We now know that the brain uses ten different mental skills for the processing and storing of information:

| Right cortex | Left cortex |
|---|---|
| pictures | numbers |
| imagination | words |
| colour | logic |
| rhythm | lists |
| space | details |

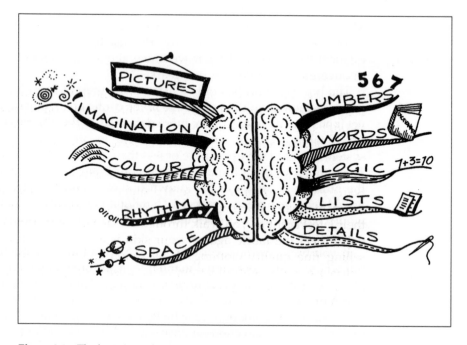

**Figure 3.1**   The brain's cerebral cortex shown face-on

# The functions of your brain

Your brain has five principal functions (see Figure 3.2). These are:

1  **Receiving**: taking in anything picked up by our five senses – sound, sight, smell, taste and touch.
2  **Holding**: this is your memory. It includes your ability to store and recall information.
3  **Analysing**: forming recognizable patterns and processing stored information.
4  **Outputting**: any form of communicating through the five senses or creative acts which include thinking, music, poetry, art and so on.
5  **Controlling**: the direction of all mental and physical functions.

These five functions all reinforce each other provided you understand the key – namely, interest. If you are interested in a subject, it will be easier to take in through your senses, easier to store, easier to analyse and use to create new data, easier to access and easier to communicate. This synergy will result in a high-performance brain. In the context of selling, the more interested you are in your customer, product, market, company and yourself, the easier it will be to sell. This one truth can revolutionize your whole approach to your sales career.

# Salesenses

Remember that your customers share the same five brain functions and are using these to make buying decisions. They absorb your sales presentation through one or a combination of their senses (function 1). The more of their senses you can engage, the better are your chances of being remembered (functions 1 and 2).

Think for a moment how your senses are engaged in the sales process. Being given a sample of cheese in a supermarket may cause you to make an unanticipated purchase of cheese. Marketers of perfume spray you with their latest scent as you walk through the department store. Encouraging you to feel the fabric against your skin is a common sales closer when selling fine quality clothing. A television commercial for a Caribbean cruise uses both sights of a tropical paradise to delight the eye and sounds of music, laughter and popping champagne bottles to please the ear.

**Figure 3.2** The five functions of the brain

# The salesenses analysis sheet

To help you analyse how to apply all the senses in your sales presentations we are including the salesenses analysis sheet. First, study the example, shown in Figure 3.3, of Ian Broderick, a hairstylist in Plumstead, London, who has used all five senses to quadruple his commissions on hair products while styling customers' hair. Then complete the blank analysis sheet (Figure 3.4) for your own product or service by carefully thinking through how to engage all of your prospect's senses at your next sales presentation.

ITEM: Hairstylist: by Ian Broderick, Plumstead, London

| Trigger | Senses |
| --- | --- |
| Sound | Playing the correct music in the salon. Not too fast or slow – something which makes the customer relax without falling asleep. |
| Sight | Showing the customer how good her hair will look. Suggest a new style. |
| Smell | The smell of the shampoos and conditioners. |
| Taste | Many hair products smell of fruit: 'You can almost taste the bananas in this shampoo, Madam.' |
| Touch | 'Feel what a difference this conditioner has made to the texture of your hair.' |

**Figure 3.3**   Example of salesenses analysis sheet

| ITEM: | | |
|---|---|---|
| **Trigger** | **Senses** | |
| **Sound** | | |
| **Sight** | | |
| **Smell** | | |
| **Taste** | | |
| **Touch** | | |

**Figure 3.4**  Salesenses analysis sheet

# The Sales Mind Matrix

In our previous book *Brain Sell* we introduced readers to the Sales Mind Matrix. Since then, through our training workshops, we have developed an analysis sheet to help implement it.

The Sales Mind Matrix is designed to cover all ten mental skills in the sales presentation (see Figure 3.5) so that customers receive a complete whole-brain picture of the product or service being sold. You might consider shading in, on the Sales Mind Matrix, the percentage for each of the ten mental skills you believe you are using in your current sales presentation.

Let's consider how each of these mental skills can apply to our everyday sales:

- *Numbers* are used for prices, discounts and keeping records.
- *Words* are used in sales conversations and in advertising: you use words to convey your sales message.

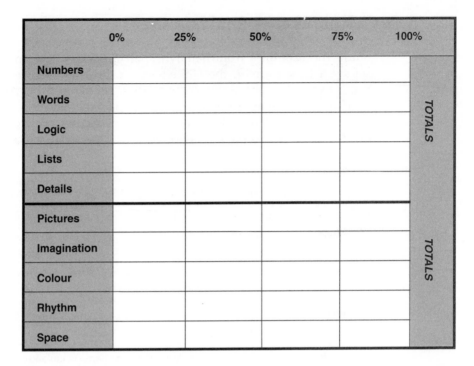

|  | 0% | 25% | 50% | 75% | 100% |  |
|---|---|---|---|---|---|---|
| Numbers |  |  |  |  |  | TOTALS |
| Words |  |  |  |  |  | |
| Logic |  |  |  |  |  | |
| Lists |  |  |  |  |  | |
| Details |  |  |  |  |  | |
| Pictures |  |  |  |  |  | TOTALS |
| Imagination |  |  |  |  |  | |
| Colour |  |  |  |  |  | |
| Rhythm |  |  |  |  |  | |
| Space |  |  |  |  |  | |

**Figure 3.5**   The Sales Mind Matrix

- *Logic* should always be present in your sale. The first logical step in the sales presentation is the greeting or gaining the customer's attention.
- *Lists* are used for prices, sizes and references. Lists help keep track and give order to the masses of information you handle.
- *Details* are important to ensure that customers receive exactly the information they want. Details can be sizes, colours and specifications.
- *Pictures* are used in sales catalogues and advertisements. Good salespeople are able to paint pictures in their customers' minds.
- *Imagination* is used when your customers picture using and enjoying your product or service in the future.
- *Colour* can be used in packaging, catalogues, advertisements and, of course, in colourful sales presentations.
- *Rhythm* can refer to the rhythm of the sales conversation where the salesperson and the customer seem to be in synchronization. You can use the rhythm of your voice to make it both interesting to listen to and memorable.
- *Space* has many different meanings. In advertising this could be the layout – one that is not too cramped and is easy to read. In face-to-face selling it could be the distance between the customer and the salesperson.

# The Sales Mind Matrix analysis sheet

Study the examples from hairstylist Ian Broderick and an approach to selling a Saturn car in the United States shown in Figures 3.6 and 3.7 respectively. We chose Saturn as it has been rated by American car purchasers as the most satisfying car-buying experience.

A blank Sales Mind Matrix analysis sheet follows (Figure 3.8). Fill this out for your own product and/or service. Once completed, you will be

| ITEM: Hairstylist: With permission of Ian Broderick, London | |
| --- | --- |
| **Trigger** | **Facts** |
| **Numbers** | The prices of services. Answer customer question, 'How many people are having this hairstyle?' |
| **Words** | We talk from the moment the customer sits in the chair until she leaves. |
| **Logic** | 'Good morning, Mrs Smith, my name is Ian and I will be doing your hair today.' Sounds ridiculous but I can count on one hand the number of hairstylists who introduce themselves. |
| **Lists** | Price lists, product information sheets and so on. |
| **Details** | Types of products to be used. Hair length and style. |
| **Pictures** | I show the customer the most commercial and most achievable picture of a style as possible. |
| **Imagination** | Follows from pictures. The client already imagines how attractive she looks, the effect it will have on her life and is probably mentally in Harrods buying a new outfit. |
| **Colour** | Hair colour, beauty treatments, make up. |
| **Rhythm** | The way you move and appear to customer. Your confidence level has to be projected so that the customer feels calm. |
| **Space** | Observe the client. Be sure to keep a comfortable distance between you. |

**Figure 3.6**   Sales Mind Matrix analysis sheet: example 1

| ITEM: SATURN (US most satisfying car-buying experience) |
| --- |

| Trigger | Facts |
| --- | --- |
| Numbers | Describe prices, styles, warranty 3 years/36 000 miles. |
| Words | Explain ranges, colours, optional equipment and owner protection plan. |
| Logic | Create a Saturn sales presentation from greeting, establishing needs, presenting range, published price list, test drive, answering questions and closing. |
| Lists | Give order to prices, styles and options. |
| Details | Describe features, technical data, safety, exterior finish, comfort and convenience, audio systems, engine/electrical, transmission and body/suspension/chassis. |
| Pictures | Show models, colours, accessories and interiors. Paint word pictures: 'Peel back that glossy skin and you'll be sitting in a reinforced steel passenger car – the formidable Saturn spaceframe.' |
| Imagination | Give history of development of Saturn and the Saturn car club for Saturnites! |
| Colour | Show range of colours for models, accessories and interiors. |
| Rhythm | Gain attention (most satisfying buying experience), be outstanding (Saturn car club), lots of YOU appeal (24-hour free road service), the end (no pressure!). Salesperson in synchronization with the buyer's needs. |
| Space | Experience the vehicle in the test drive, the boot, the leg room and the handling. Allow the customer mental space (no pressure!). |

**Figure 3.7**   Sales Mind Matrix analysis sheet: example 2

able to include this remarkable tool in future sales conversations, ensuring that you cover all your customers' cortical skills!

# The Brain Sell Grid

To make the salesenses and Sales Mind Matrix easy for you to use and

| ITEM: | | |
|-------|---|---|
| **Trigger** | **Facts** | |
| **Numbers** | | |
| **Words** | | |
| **Logic** | | |
| **Lists** | | |
| **Details** | | |
| **Pictures** | | |
| **Imagination** | | |
| **Colour** | | |
| **Rhythm** | | |
| **Space** | | |

**Figure 3.8**   Sales Mind Matrix analysis sheet

apply to all aspects of your developing Sales Genius, we have combined them in the Brain Sell Grid. A blank copy, for you to duplicate and complete, follows the analysis sheets (see Figure 3.9).

# Summary

In this chapter we have reviewed the latest research on the brain. We also took an in-depth look at how this applies to selling, including:

- the functions of your brain
- salesenses – what you hear, see, smell, taste and touch
- the salesenses analysis sheet
- the Sales Mind Matrix's ten mental skills
  - numbers
  - words

- logic
- lists
- details
- pictures
- imagination
- colour
- rhythm
- space
- the Sales Mind Matrix analysis sheet
- the Brain Sell Grid.

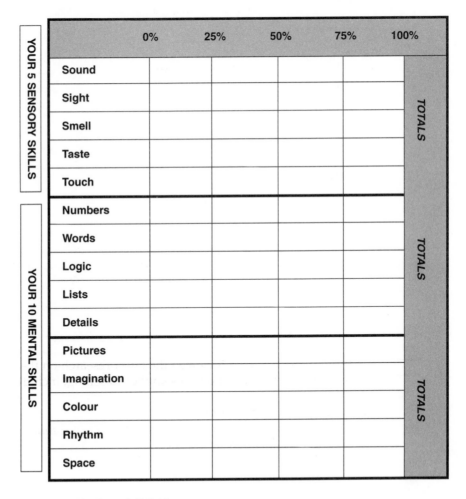

Figure 3.9  The Brain Sell Grid

# 4    Sales intelligences

In Chapter 3 we explored the five functions of the brain. Next we looked in detail at function no. 1 – how the customer receives your information through their five senses. We also examined the ten cortical skills that make up the building-blocks of our thinking. How you use and develop these skills determines how effectively you optimize your intelligence. It was thought until recently that we had two principal intelligences – mathematical/logical and verbal. However, it has now been established through the pioneering work of Professor Howard Gardner of Harvard University that there are many types of intelligence. For *Sales Genius* we have selected 12 types of intelligence that we consider to be critical to sales success.

## Intelligence profile questionnaire

What is your intelligence profile? Read each statement and see how well it expresses your own personal characteristics, circling the answer as true, unsure or false as applicable.

| | Statement | True | Unsure | False |
|---|---|---|---|---|
| 1 | My first impressions of people turn out to be accurate. | 2 | 1 | 0 |
| 2 | I approach every sales presentation the same way: I qualify, sell benefits, overcome objections and attempt to close. | 2 | 1 | 0 |
| 3 | I'd rather have a map to a client's address than verbal directions. | 2 | 1 | 0 |
| 4 | When I make or lose a sale, I am either happy or angry. | 2 | 1 | 0 |
| 5 | I can play a musical instrument. | 2 | 1 | 0 |
| 6 | I enjoy entertaining friends for parties or dinners. | 2 | 1 | 0 |
| 7 | I like to work with calculators and/or computers. | 2 | 1 | 0 |
| 8 | When the doorbell or telephone rings unexpectedly, I know who it is. | 2 | 1 | 0 |
| 9 | I can speak spontaneously to my clients. | 2 | 1 | 0 |
| 10 | I have excellent powers of observation. | 2 | 1 | 0 |
| 11 | I learn new dance steps easily. | 2 | 1 | 0 |
| 12 | I can detect and respond to my customers' feelings. | 2 | 1 | 0 |
| 13 | When customers raise objections, I have good answers. | 2 | 1 | 0 |
| 14 | I like crosswords, Scrabble and similar games. | 2 | 1 | 0 |
| 15 | I am very convincing with clients. | 2 | 1 | 0 |
| 16 | I enjoy going to the cinema. | 2 | 1 | 0 |
| 17 | I am good at seeing patterns and relationships between numbers. | 2 | 1 | 0 |
| 18 | I find it easy to ride a bike and/or (roller) skate. | 2 | 1 | 0 |
| 19 | When I analyse an error in judgement, I can remember feeling slightly uneasy at the time about my decision. | 2 | 1 | 0 |
| 20 | Music adds richness to my life. | 2 | 1 | 0 |
| 21 | I appreciate listening to good sales conversations. | 2 | 1 | 0 |
| 22 | I have always had a good rapport with people. | 2 | 1 | 0 |
| 23 | When travelling to a client's address, I have the directions in my head. | 2 | 1 | 0 |
| 24 | I have a good memory for everything I have tasted. | 2 | 1 | 0 |

**Cont'd**

| Statement | True | Unsure | False |
|---|---|---|---|
| 25  I can hear conversations from the other side of a noisy room. | 2 | 1 | 0 |
| 26  I know exactly how to behave when I encounter a difficult sales situation. | 2 | 1 | 0 |
| 27  I can often associate a piece of music to an event in my life. | 2 | 1 | 0 |
| 28  I like to draw pictures while talking on the telephone. | 2 | 1 | 0 |
| 29  I can fix car engines or other motors. | 2 | 1 | 0 |
| 30  I can picture the best way to make a sales presentation. | 2 | 1 | 0 |
| 31  I'm annoyed by clients who talk nonsense. | 2 | 1 | 0 |
| 32  I have a good sense of balance and coordination. | 2 | 1 | 0 |
| 33  I can find my way around new places. | 2 | 1 | 0 |
| 34  I can study diagrams or specifications with ease. | 2 | 1 | 0 |
| 35  I can easily follow the instructions for new electronic equipment or electrical appliances. | 2 | 1 | 0 |
| 36  I can clearly see solutions to sales situations. | 2 | 1 | 0 |
| 37  I dream about unusual events that actually happen later. | 2 | 1 | 0 |
| 38  I can always devise innovative ways to obtain new customers. | 2 | 1 | 0 |
| 39  I am sensitive to the moods of others. | 2 | 1 | 0 |
| 40  I have a mental picture of my sales goals. | 2 | 1 | 0 |
| 41  I am good at judging distances. | 2 | 1 | 0 |
| 42  I can identify the names of different colognes and perfumes from their smell. | 2 | 1 | 0 |
| 43  I am good at remembering customers' faces. | 2 | 1 | 0 |
| 44  When it comes to planning a sales presentation I always make a plan either in my head or on paper. | 2 | 1 | 0 |
| 45  I sing or hum when I'm alone. | 2 | 1 | 0 |
| 46  I am good at making up and telling stories. | 2 | 1 | 0 |
| 47  I can mentally cheer myself up when I'm feeling low. | 2 | 1 | 0 |

**Cont'd**

| Statement | True | Unsure | False |
|---|---|---|---|
| 48   I am good at improvising. | 2 | 1 | 0 |
| 49   I have an instinct for when a customer is going to buy. | 2 | 1 | 0 |
| 50   I enjoying using my hands at work. | 2 | 1 | 0 |
| 51   I have a good vocabulary and like to learn new words. | 2 | 1 | 0 |
| 52   I'm good at solving puzzles. | 2 | 1 | 0 |
| 53   I enjoy taking measurements or drawing up plans for clients. | 2 | 1 | 0 |
| 54   I am able to change moods for different occasions. | 2 | 1 | 0 |
| 55   I have control over my emotions. | 2 | 1 | 0 |
| 56   I have a system of following up prospects and customers that I keep to. | 2 | 1 | 0 |
| 57   I like different music for different moods. | 2 | 1 | 0 |
| 58   I enjoy taking part in different sporting activities. | 2 | 1 | 0 |
| 59   I enjoy writing, and write my own sales letters. | 2 | 1 | 0 |
| 60   I have a good idea of what others think of me. | 2 | 1 | 0 |

## Scoring

Add up your scores for each of the 12 categories of intelligence, as follows.

Sensory intelligence      Score: _____
Questions: 10, 24, 25, 33, 42

Intuitive intelligence      Score: _____
Questions: 1, 8, 19, 37, 49

Logical intelligence      Score: _____
Questions: 2, 14, 26, 44, 56

Verbal intelligence      Score: _____
Questions: 9, 21, 31, 51, 59

Spatial intelligence        Score: _____
Questions: 3, 23, 35, 41, 53


Personal intelligence       Score: _____
Questions: 4, 12, 47, 54, 55


Musical intelligence        Score: _____
Questions: 5, 20, 27, 45, 57


Mind–body intelligence Score: _____
Questions: 11, 18, 32, 50, 58


People intelligence         Score: _____
Questions: 6, 15, 22, 39, 60


Technical intelligence      Score: _____
Questions: 7, 17, 29, 34, 52


Visual intelligence         Score: _____
Questions: 16, 30, 36, 40, 43


Creative intelligence       Score: _____
Questions: 13, 28, 38, 46, 48


A score of eight or more indicates a very high level of the corresponding intelligence. Those on which you scored less than eight are areas of potential intelligence which, when accessed, can propel you to greater heights than you have ever before achieved.

For each of the 12 intelligences, there are activities to be found in the 100-day diary in Part Three. You can find the specific exercise activities for each intelligence by referring to the Index of Activities on page 233. However, we strongly recommend that you carry out all the activities, with special emphasis on the areas which need development.

# The 12 types of intelligence

Let's look at the different intelligences in detail and see how they relate to your sales potential.

## 1   Sensory intelligence

Sensory intelligence was covered in 'Salesenses' in Chapter 3. Leonardo da Vinci, ranked as the number one genius of all time in Tony Buzan's *Book of Genius*, wrote about ways to develop your whole creative brain. He believed this process included developing all your senses, particularly your sense of sight.

This particular sense is critical to selling. As a salesperson, you are constantly looking for clues – the customer's body language, their facial expression, what they are attracted to, personal effects in their office or how they respond to your sales conversation. All of this revolves around your ability to observe.

## 2   Intuitive intelligence

Intuition means different things to each of us. At one level it might mean letting go, at another, accessing an inner wisdom that is often obscured by the ego or an overactive and critical mind. In selling, intuition may be called by different names: gut feeling, insight, perception or even 'good judgement'.

Although often ignored or disguised, no matter what it is called and whatever its source, intuition is a necessary part of the decision-making process. At some level below consciousness, your customer is making decisions about you, your company and your offer. Opinions vary on the role played by intuition in making the final decision to buy, but there is no doubt that it is too important to be overlooked.

How, then, can you make a good impression on the client's intuitive process? As we make clear in *Brain Sell*, the client is using a truth-seeking brain – that is, a brain that wants the truth. The best advice we can give you is to be truthful and honest in all your dealings, as the client's own intuition will probably sense if you are being otherwise. There may be instances where you are puzzled as to a client's rejection of your offer despite your having made what you consider a sound presentation. The explanation could be that you were not congruent with your body language, behaviours, voice or eye contact, resulting in the client intuitively rejecting your offer.

## 3   Logical intelligence

In the 1925 British sales author E. K. Strong published the very first sales formula *The Psychology of Selling* based on a strictly logical approach to selling. Strong's premise was that customers bought benefits and, in order to achieve this, the salesperson had to use a logical approach – to establish needs, present the appropriate benefits, overcome objections and, finally, close the sale. This has been the standard model for training salespeople for the last 70 years, and it is still widely used.

Although we do not disagree with this approach, we believe it is severely limited, since it appeals only to customers who are processing logically using their left cortical skills. However, for customers who are using their whole brain or other cortical skills, this logical approach to selling misses the mark.

## 4   Verbal intelligence

Verbal intelligence is our ability to communicate with words. It is a very important aspect of selling because we place so much emphasis on the verbal presentation even though we know that the verbal part of the presentation is only one of the ten cortical skills.

There is a correlation between vocabulary and income – that is, the more words you know, the more income you are likely to have. There's no doubt about the value of investing in developing your knowledge bank of words. It will pay handsome dividends.

However, words are more than mere words. First, they can paint pictures. For example, when you think about your best friend do you just think of their name or does a picture of, or feeling about, that person come to mind? As the customer is storing your information in pictures and/or feelings, you should make those word pictures as vivid as possible.

Second, carefully chosen words can become powerful sales tools when constructed as stories about your product or services and related at the appropriate time. For example, we all know that a whole industry – that of public relations – has been built around selling appropriate stories about their clients to the right media at the right time. Watch any TV commercial and you will see and hear a story being told about products and services in creative and imaginative ways. Stories are selling millions of pounds' worth of products every minute: this means that you need a few good stories of your own.

In constructing your story, use the Brain Sell Grid as a checklist to ensure that your story is appealing to all of your customer's cortical skills.

## 5   Spatial intelligence

 Spatial intelligence is the ability to judge distance and time in such a way that your customer is more receptive to you and you become more memorable to him or her. Athletes know the importance of spatial intelligence. Those who have spatial intelligence perfected can make huge salaries as golfers, basketball or soccer players and the like.

There are many ways of using spatial intelligence. In selling, it can relate to the distance between you and your client. Richard Israel terms this space 'the last four feet' – not too far to be distant and not too close to be intimate. Your spatial intelligence should tell you exactly when you are in this zone.

Many studies have been carried out in retail relating to customer flow and merchandise display. Boots, Marks and Spencer and Bloomingdale's have perfected the use of spatial intelligence. Customers feel comfortable shopping in these stores which take pains not to make the customer feel too cramped nor to make the merchandise appear too sparse.

Perimeter Mall in Atlanta was the first to discover that they could place push carts selling merchandise in the middle of customer traffic flow through their open areas. Customers found this arrangement tremendously appealing, and this concept is now becoming popular worldwide. Being able to walk around the push cart and see all the merchandise in a 360-degree swoop, as opposed to entering a store and struggling to see even part of the selection, encourages impulse buying. The whole concept is based on spatial awareness.

Spatial awareness in long-cycle selling, where you have to make more than one presentation or call to close the sale, refers to the spacing of follow-up calls. To make sure they are remembered by the customer, salespeople should keep to the following follow-up sequence: 24 hours, seven days and one month, as described in Chapter 7, p. 71.

## 6   Personal intelligence

 Personal intelligence concerns how you manage yourself! We have approximately 40 000 thoughts each day. What is the quality of those thoughts? The quality of those thoughts impact on both your behaviour and your success and enjoyment in life. If most of your thoughts are negative, your behaviours and results will also be negative. However, once you understand that you can manage your thinking process, you are well on the way to developing your personal intelligence. Understanding yourself, your thinking, behaviour and moods will result in your being a far more balanced and happier person.

Customers are attracted to salespeople who are both positive and enthusiastic. Would you want to buy anything from a depressed, unmotivated, uninterested salesperson? It is therefore of paramount importance that you gain as much insight as possible into your own thinking processes and behaviours.

One of the best ways of doing this is by keeping a daily diary in which you note your thinking and behaviours for that day. This allows you to reflect and learn from what is happening to you on a frequent, ongoing basis. You may well discover in this process that there are certain incidents, customers or situations which trigger negative or positive changes in your mood or behaviour. For example, how do you handle rejection? Do you regard it as a rejection of you as a person or of the product or service that you offer? There's a world of difference. A feeling of personal rejection can result in low self-esteem as well as a reluctance to make further calls.

If, on the other hand, you view rejection as feedback, you are in a continuous state of learning and can develop new strategies for success. This can be an empowering and enlightening process.

These simple observation techniques – that is, recording daily in a diary, reflecting and analysing and adapting new thinking and behaviour patterns – can prove immeasurably helpful in your quest to improve your sales performance.

## 7   Musical intelligence

Musical intelligence revolves around your appreciation for music and rhythm, not necessarily your talent for it. If you enjoy background music, find yourself humming or whistling a favourite tune or enjoying a musical show, you are using your musical intelligence.

From time immemorial, music has been used by every known religion and society in some rhythmic way to place prayers into people's long-term memory. In many cultures where people are unable to read, long texts are memorized simply by a rhythmic, repetitious pattern of singing or chanting. You may remember from your kindergarten days how you used music to learn to count or add.

In selling, music and rhythm are used in various ways. Consider all the advertising jingles from radio and TV commercials that lodge in your memory whether you like it or not! Think about your favourite salesperson and play back their voice in your mind. Is it a dull, monotonous voice or one that has inflection, rhythm and musical qualities? Most likely it's the latter, because dull, boring, monotonous voices send sales prospects to sleep.

How does your voice measure up? You need to listen to your voice objectively, and the best way to do this is to make a few tape recordings of yourself in actual sales situations. You should also include a tape recording of yourself on the telephone, as telephone selling relies 90 per cent on voice! Once you have the recording, analyse it not only for content and flow but also for interest. Ask yourself: 'Is it a voice I would like to listen to? How can I make my voice more musical?'

Listening to voices that appeal to you and deciding what makes those voices interesting can be a significant learning experience. By using your sensory intelligence to improve your musical intelligence, you will be creating a synergistic effect.

Every sales presentation has a certain rhythm or 'dance' to it. Being in harmony with your customer puts you into a sales flow that often ends in a successful outcome.

## 8   Mind–body intelligence

The mind and the body are inseparably linked. The way you approach each day will have a direct effect on your energy level. If you wake up feeling tired, that you hate your job and that you aren't well enough rested, you will be physically dragging all day long. If, on the other hand, you awaken with the attitude that this is going to be a great day, you will feel energized. No matter how smart you are, if you don't take good care of your physical health and pay attention to what your body is telling you, you will not have the vigour and energy required to be successful in sales. Selling can produce stress. You can choose to defuse that stress in an unhealthy manner such as through alcohol, smoking or excess eating, or you can choose to take physical exercise. When you keep your body in good physical condition you have more energy and experience less stress. In addition, you will look better, which can improve your self-confidence.

Part of good physical care includes sensible eating. Keep your fat and calorie intake low and consume plenty of fruit, vegetables and water to maintain a healthy body and appearance. Even though your job may require eating out frequently in restaurants, do not use this as an excuse to eat the wrong foods. Choose from the menu carefully.

Body language is another crucial component of success. Standing up to greet a customer shows enthusiasm for that person and your job. Standing tall communicates confidence. Looking the customer straight in the eye makes you appear sincere. Conversely, slouching, failure to stand up, avoiding a customer's gaze or other evasive behaviour creates an atmosphere of distrust between you and your customer and will seriously reduce your chances of a successful outcome. Ask a friend to videotape you interacting with others in a social or business setting. As you view this tape, analyse your body language and ask your friend to comment on what you are doing right and how you can improve.

It's interesting to note, over the last ten years, the growing interest in the mind–body connection. An analysis of popular magazines shows an unprecedented number of articles on the subject. Almost every popular magazine features a mind–body article at least once each year. Health clubs everywhere offer yoga, meditation and other pursuits which involve both mind and body.

## 9   People intelligence

People intelligence is the ability to build a rapport with others and, as every salesperson knows, this is the critical skill in a successful selling career. Countless books and courses are available on this important subject.

There are various schools of thought on how to improve your people intelligence. One school of thought maintains that, since enthusiasm is contagious, you should be enthusiastic about your product, service and company and your customer will begin to feel the same way. Diametrically opposed to this is a school of thought which teaches you to mirror your customer's posture, energy level and speech pattern in order to become synchronized. We believe that you must decide which approach suits your personality and that of your customer and be adaptable.

There are two critical questions to ask yourself. How do I make someone like me and how do I make someone trust me? Without these two ingredients of liking and trust it is difficult to reach your sales objectives.

To be liked and trusted you must be perceived as being sincere, honest and reliable. You must always be sensitive to your customer's current situation, paying attention to the sound of their voice and body language. Are they stressed, hurried or distracted? If so, back off. Conversely, do they need more information or a little more encouragement to make a decision? If so, be a little more assertive. How many salespeople do you know who won't take 'no' for an answer? These people have no insight into their behaviour. They believe that by bullying the customer they are increasing their chances of making a sale. Even though this might work in some instances, the customer often experiences 'buyer's remorse' and vows never to deal with that salesperson or their product/service again. This type of behaviour is the opposite of personal intelligence and does not promote repeat business. It's like going into a restaurant and being persuaded by a waiter to eat fish even though you have told the waiter you do not like it. You may eat the fish but you will probably be reluctant to return to that restaurant or, at the very least, to be attended to by that particular waiter.

## 10   Technical intelligence

 Alvin Toffler in his book *The Third Wave* describes the third wave as the information explosion, driven by technology. Technology plays an increasing role in every aspect of our lives, especially in the area of communications. Where would we be without fax machines, mobile phones, computers, e-mail and the Internet, all of which are communicating information from one source to another? As salespeople, we are in exactly the same business – communicating information from one source to another, in this case from ourselves to our customers.

So important is the need for technical knowledge on how to use a computer that 90 per cent of advertised jobs in the United States require computer literacy. The message is clear. If you are to be part of the new economy, you *must* be computer literate. On our travels we are always surprised to find organizations that are reluctant to make this transition, where sales teams still have no access to the tools of the computer age. This attitude places their whole company's future in jeopardy.

Technical knowledge is not only crucial to your personal success; the more you know about the technology relating to your particular industry, the greater an asset you become to your company.

In the late 1960s Tony Buzan invented a technique known as Mind Mapping. Throughout his organization Mind Maps have been used exclusively for a whole range of business practices. Until 1998 these Mind Maps had always been created by hand. With the advent of MindManager, a Mind Map software program, members of the organization were now able not only to store their Mind Maps on their computers but to send their Mind Maps to other members of the organization worldwide. This represented a significant leap in both the speed and effectiveness of communication within the Buzan organization and has added dramatically to its knowledge pool and intellectual capital.

## 11   Visual intelligence

 In the human brain, part of memory comprises pictures made up from all five senses (functions 1 and 2 in Chapter 3). When you leave your customer after making a sales presentation, ask yourself: 'How memorable was that presentation?' After all, your customer is probably inundated with other buying opportunities. The challenge is to make *your* presentation the most memorable and persuasive.

Customers take in information visually. The visual part of your presentation plays a far more important role than the verbal (what you say). In the way you are dressed, your mannerisms, behaviour, sales aids and advertising materials, you are like an artist painting a picture of yourself. We can't overemphasize the importance of visual impact. That's why face-to-face contact has always been crucial in closing sales. You need to match your customer's expectations with appropriate dress, behaviour and presentation.

While you wouldn't expect your bank manager to wear bermuda shorts and a T-shirt at work, this might well be appropriate dress for a boat seller. To make a positively memorable visual impression your materials should be orderly, organized, accessible, complete and as high quality as possible. Use colour whenever possible, even if it costs more. Colour is more mentally stimulating. Paint word pictures of what your product/service will do for your client. For example, a travel agent selling an African safari holiday might say, 'You will wake up in your safari lodge to the sounds of roebucks, antelopes, birds, lions and hippos making their way down to breakfast at the nearby watering hole. As the red sun creeps over the horizon and your naked feet touch the warm, red African soil you will also feel the soft, balmy air against your skin. It's an experience you will always remember.' This use of multisensory language builds strong, memorable word pictures in your customer's mind.

Probably the best method of checking your visual presentation is through videotaping. Study the playback for both visual and auditory elements; ask yourself the key question: 'Am I making this memorable?'

## 12   Creative intelligence

Selling, by its very nature, requires creative intelligence. Every day is different, bringing new challenges, many of which require creative answers. How do you find new clients? How do you overcome competitors? How do you find new ways to promote yourself and your products/services? Simply repeating everything you have done over the previous days, weeks and months can only produce the same results. It's creativity in selling that produces the breakthroughs – new products, new ideas, new markets, new clients, new companies and new industries.

It was once thought that the mental skills found in the right hemisphere – that is, colour, imagination, rhythm, space and pictures – were responsible for creativity. Now we know that it is the combination of both left and right cortical skills working together that results in the whole creative brain. Therefore, the more use you can make of all of your cortical skills, the more creative you can be.

If you are a car salesperson, try a totally new activity such as taking an art class. It will help you sell more cars. This may sound ridiculous, but it is the key to increasing your whole creative brain because it is activating cortical skills you don't normally use. Because art is, by its nature, creative it will stimulate your brain to be creative in other areas of your life, including your work.

We both work with a world-renowned artist, Conni Gordon, who is hired by Fortune 500 companies to teach their top sales teams how to paint! Why would they do this and pay her $10 000 a day, plus expenses? Because the pay-off in increased creativity for those sales forces is enormous. Conni uses a whole-brain process to teach art that is quite remarkable. We asked her permission to reproduce her technique in this book for you. We will end this chapter by allowing you to experience the Conni Gordon Four-Step Method to creative thinking.

# The Conni Gordon Four-Step Method®

To experience your creative intelligence, first benchmark where you think you are now. In the space below draw a landscape, including sky, hills, water and trees.

Do the best you possibly can.

Do not turn the page until you have completed this activity.

My landscape BC (Before Conni)

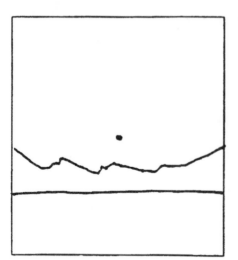

**Step 1: Outline**

Use a pen or pencil. Start with a dot in the centre. Divide the space as follows. Halfway between the dot and the bottom of the box, draw a horizontal straight line. In between, add a slanted, uneven mountain range.

**Step 2: Support**

Let the white paper be the support for your sky area. Use light pressure to slant mountain lines. Use heavier pressure to draw water lines. Don't fill in completely.

**Step 3: Form**

Freely sketch uneven bushes across the bottom of the mountain range. Draw and darken an 'S'-shaped tree trunk down from top to bottom of box. Add shorter tapered 'Y'-shaped branches.

**Step 4: Details**

Scribble three separate dark uneven curved leaf-shapes across tree. Add more branches. Then fill in the bottom ground area solidly. Add curved weeds. Initial and date your 'masterpiece'. WOW!

Follow the instructions appearing on page 54 to complete your masterpiece.

My landscape AC (After Conni)

# Applying the Conni Gordon Four-Step Method to creativity

This four-step method is designed to teach you how to think creatively.

- **Step 1: Outline**. Forming an outline creates the 'big picture'. It answers the question 'What do I want to create?' Once you decide, keep this picture in your mind.
- **Step 2: Support**. What supports, options or skills do you have? Once you start to consider this, you'll be surprised how many you do have. Start to link, connect and associate these to your 'big picture'.
- **Step 3: Form**. This is the 'how-to' or 'process' step. It contains the 'creative leap' or the 'A-Ha!' in which the whole idea takes form. This might not happen immediately, so be prepared to wait. Your creative brain is searching for the shape it will take and this might emerge today, tomorrow or in a few days' time.
- **Step 4: Details**. What details unite for success? Once you have the form (Step 3) you are ready to fill in the details. Remember, every detail counts.

In the same way as you completed your artistic masterpiece on the previous page – a truly creative accomplishment – so you can now apply the four-step process to create solutions to other situations that you face.

# Summary

In this chapter we examined the 12 intelligences that make up a Sales Genius:

- sensory
- intuitive
- logical
- verbal
- spatial
- personal

- musical
- mind–body
- people
- technical
- visual
- creative.

The quiz enabled you to ascertain your strengths and those areas that need improvement, and the Conni Gordon Four-Step Method developed creative thinking.

By now, you should have thought of new ideas to improve your sales performance.

# PART TWO

## What makes a successful sale?

# 5 Away from pain and towards pleasure

## Pain

Have you ever had the experience of waking up with a toothache on a Thursday? It hurts but isn't that bad, so you do nothing about it. It's still around on Friday and, again, you choose not to call the dentist. Come Sunday morning, however, the pain is so acute that you can't eat or drink. Finally, you are motivated to call the dentist and you're willing to pay anything – *anything* – to have that tooth fixed NOW!!!

Of course it's Sunday and no dentists are available. You will have to wait until Monday, so you walk around in absolute misery! Your current reality or 'present picture' is one of unremitting pain. When you think of Monday, with a fixed tooth and no pain, that's your 'future picture'.

The above exemplifies a major principle that applies to all prospects and customers. In fact, it applies to all of us whether we are planning a holiday, acting as a salesperson or being a customer – the desire to move *away* from *pain*.

The more intense the *pain*, the more prospects and/or customers are motivated to have the pain removed! This is a primary motive to buy – *away* from *pain*!

The term 'pain' encompasses a wide range of feelings – everything from wanting to buy something to make the house less gloomy to desiring to keep up with the Joneses to facing the risk of severe medical or health consequences.

# Pleasure

Let's change the pictures! You are planning your next holiday. You spend a good deal of time discussing with your partner where you want to go, what sort of experiences, foods, sights and adventures you desire. You speak to friends who have been to your chosen destination, visit travel agents and read travel guides. Your anticipation of the pleasure rises continuously as you think about the 'future picture' – the holiday.

You have invested time, energy and resources in imagining how pleasurable this holiday will turn out to be. Where you are now is your current reality, your 'present picture'. The 'future picture' is one of enjoying the holiday. This illustration introduces the next motive to buy! People, prospects and customers want to move *towards pleasure*.

Whatever a person is interested in buying can be pictured as *away* from pain, the 'present picture', and/or *towards pleasure*, the 'future picture'.

## Motivation: the buying pull

Customers buy when the pull or motivation between the two pictures (present and future) is strong enough. In the case of the toothache, the motivator, or pull, is removing the *pain*. In the case of the holiday, the motivator, or pull, is obtaining *pleasure*.

You need to establish both the present and future pictures to intensify the pull – that degree of *pain* or *pleasure*. The stronger the pull, the more likely it is that the customer will buy. Salespersons and customers must share the same pictures. In many instances the customer is unaware of the present or future pictures and therefore cannot identify the pull or motivation to move from the 'present picture' to the 'future picture'. It's the salesperson's skill in establishing these two distinct pictures in the prospective customer's mind and the intensity of the pull – away from *pain* or towards *pleasure* – that makes for a successful sale. Think back to the toothache example.

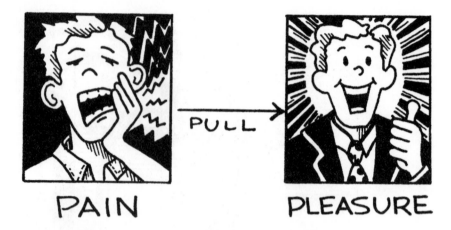

PAIN                              PLEASURE

On Sunday when the pain was unbearable and there was no dentist available, you were prepared to pay almost anything to have a dentist fix that tooth!

Now reflect on television commercials. They must tell their stories in 10, 30 or 60 seconds. For maximum impact, a good commercial uses a whole creative brain approach – that is, music, pictures, colour and as many of the cortical skills as possible. It also takes advantage of the perceived 'pull' for viewers – it offers something to improve their life, appeal to their vanity or allay their fears. It illustrates one of the most potent forms of selling yet devised to appeal to a mass market!

The TV commercial has to create both the 'present picture' and the 'future picture' in the viewers' minds! The present picture might be a man exercising and worrying that he has body odour. Then he's shown using a deodorant soap and, in the next scene, a beautiful woman is embracing him. The motivator – away from *pain* and/or towards *pleasure* – has been rapidly established. He's worried about being offensive, he takes action, then he finds out he's not offensive. In fact, he is even attractive! The stronger that pull and association with the viewer, the more successful the outcome in terms of sales.

As you can imagine, this is some challenge! Yet watching commercials and analysing how they are constructed can be an extremely effective learning tool for selling. Commercials often cost significant sums of money to both make and broadcast. Yet that money is well spent when the cash registers start to ring!

PAIN                                    PLEASURE

## Applications

Do you have hunger pains? Visit a restaurant. Are you concerned about your car breaking down on the motorway? Then join the AA. Do you want the pleasure of impressing your friends with a posh new car? Visit an upmarket car showroom. Do you want to avoid the worry of not having enough income in the future? Build your pension plan. Do you want to have a great figure? Then join a health club. We could go on and on, but the message is that we are motivated to move *away* from *pain* and *towards pleasure*.

## Summary

In this chapter we covered how to motivate people to buy.

- Customers want to move away from pain.
- Customers want to move towards pleasure.
- Form present and future pictures in customers' minds.
- The difference between present and future pictures is the pull.
- The stronger the pull, the more intense the motive to buy.
- Customers buy in order to move away from pain towards pleasure.

# 6    Complete picture selling

## The principles

According to Steven K. Scott, author of *Simple Steps to Impossible Dreams*, there is a big difference between persuasion and manipulation. He says:

> Manipulation is using any means necessary to motivate or force a person to do something that fulfils YOUR desire or need, whether or not it is in his or her best interest (the focus is the desire or benefit of the manipulator, not the benefit of the person being manipulated).
>
> Persuasion is the art of guiding one's mind through a field of ignorance, misinformation or misunderstanding to a destination where there is enough information and understanding to make a logical choice to do that which is in the best interest of the person being persuaded.

Customers have a truth-seeking brain, as we explained in our book, *Brain Sell*. Customers want the truth! Using this knowledge, the principles of the complete picture method are based on finding out the customer's true motivation or desires so that you can offer them the best product or service for their needs.

Having established this, you can then be proactive in determining whether you have hit the nail on the head and take whatever steps are necessary to be more on target. A good salesperson is able to identify their customer's position and then go into action to meet their needs or desires.

An unethical salesperson can temporarily create a pull on the part of a potential customer and realize a sale, but ultimately this will backfire and discourage the customer from doing future business with him or her.

## The complete picture method

We introduced the complete picture method briefly in *Brain Sell*. Here, we advised readers to develop completed, shared brain pictures of their customers' needs. We explained that this could be achieved by asking detective questions. We will now cover the complete picture method in detail, including the different types of question you need to ask. But, first, what is a sale?

*A sale takes place when the salesperson and the potential customer share a common 'future picture' and the product or service offered matches that 'future picture'.*

This means that you need to establish with customers as soon as possible what they are looking for (their 'future picture') and how this will change or improve their current situation. In other words, what 'pain' has brought them to the point of enquiring about this new product or service and what 'pleasure' do they seek to achieve by means of the change?

If you are selling cars and the customer says, 'Oh, I'm just a bit tired of my car. I don't know if I am ready to buy another one or not', you might explore this statement in order to obtain a fuller picture – and thus the extent of their motivation to buy a new car.

Ask such questions as: 'Have you been having mechanical problems with your car?'; 'Do you like the newer models better?'; 'Do you think a new car would better suit your image?' If you receive a positive response to any of these questions you can assume that there was some sort of pull that brought them into your showroom. If you get no sense whatsoever of any pull, then this person may, in fact, simply be window shopping, and you can react accordingly.

If, on the other hand, you learn that this person has had the car in for repairs three times in the last four weeks, there's clear, unmistakable pain which can be relieved through the purchase of a new car. Nevertheless, handing over a large sum of money in the form of car payments creates a spectre of future pain unless you point out that car payments are insignificant compared to the security of knowing that the car isn't going to break down on a dark rainy night.

Without insulting their intelligence by talking down to the customer, paint a future picture of pleasure such as how good they would feel driving a new car, how it would enhance their business image or how the added security of a dependable car would give them relief.

The more specifically you create the 'future picture' of *away* from pain and/or *towards* pleasure in your customer's mind, the more pull or motivation you stimulate in the customer to achieve that 'future picture'.

# Present and future questions

First establish the 'present picture'. There are two ways to do this: through personal observation and by asking questions. Take note of anything visible to the eye – for example, worn tyres, rust, a car that is 10 years old. There are two types of question you can use at this stage: present questions and future questions.

*Present questions*   are questions that help build up a picture of the current situation. They ask about the present circumstances and the problem – the pain – being experienced: 'Have you been having mechanical problems with your car?'

*Future questions*   are any questions that help build up the 'future picture' containing pleasure: 'Do you like the newer models better?'; 'Do you think a new car would better suit your image?'

# The brain fills in

Always make as few assumptions as possible because your brain craves completion in all situations and will fill in the blanks for itself when it does not receive sufficient information. For example, if a customer says she wants new furniture to upgrade her office, don't tell her, 'I have exactly what you need', because your idea of upgraded office furniture may be nothing like what she has in mind. Ask present and future questions and listen to the responses so that you can build up the complete picture.

Failing to have a complete picture causes many delays and aggravations in our lives whether we're on the 'giving' or the 'receiving' end. Have you ever described to your hairdresser the haircut you wanted only to end up with something you wouldn't have wished on your worst enemy? Have you ever bought a Christmas gift for someone, certain that it was just what they wanted, and discovered later that it had been returned? We could continue indefinitely. However, the point is that the person serving you did not share the same 'future picture' as you! When the salesperson sees an incomplete 'future picture', guess what? Their brain fills in, more often than not with the wrong details!

- 'But I wanted this in a size 11, not a size 9.'
- 'I expected my sole to be filleted, not on the bone.'
- 'New tyres? I thought you were just going to rotate the old ones.'

The above examples leave you in *pain* rather than give you *pleasure*. Our experience has shown us that a principal reason for failure to achieve a sale is that the salesperson and customer did not share the same 'future picture'.

The time you spend discussing, defining and formulating your 'future picture' with the client will be the most valuable time you can spend in any sales presentation.

# The brain devises ways to its ends

Have you ever desired something so badly that you started thinking up all sorts of ways to obtain it? That's because when you experience pull – when your creative brain has a clear goal – it will devise ways to achieve it.

In selling this works both ways. As a salesperson, if you stimulate, in your customer's mind, the present and future picture as well as the pull, your customer will start to think of ways to achieve the future picture. In the car example, if the customer likes that new blue convertible, he will want you to help him work out how to stretch the payments to suit his budget or he'll consider a savings bond that he could cash in or remember that his aunt has offered to lend him money if he ever needed it.

Once you, as the salesperson, have established the present and future picture, your creative brain also starts thinking of ways to close the sale. Can you offer to add racing stripes to the bodywork or throw in an extended warranty? The more complete and separate both the present and future pictures are, and the stronger the pull, the greater are your chances of completing the sale – particularly if you have managed to help create a strong positive picture in the customer's mind.

Here are some further examples of how to establish present and future pictures:

- 'What are your concerns now about the reliability of your equipment?' (*present question = present picture*)
- 'Would a second back-up machine give you peace of mind?' (*future question = future picture*)

- 'How do you feel about your current level of fitness?' (*present question = present picture*)
- 'What kind of condition would you like to be in in three months?' (*future question = future picture*)

Now, in the space below, make up some present and future questions you could ask for your own product and/or service.

**Present questions** are any questions that help build up the 'present picture' – the current situation containing the problem and the pain being experienced.

1 _____
2 _____
3 _____
4 _____
5 _____

**Future questions** are any questions that help build up the 'future picture' containing pleasure.

1 _____
2 _____
3 _____
4 _____
5 _____

# Summary

In this chapter we have explained the important difference between manipulation and persuasion. Because we know that the customer has a truth-seeking brain, we should always use persuasion in selling. Build a present and future picture by using your powers of observation and asking present and future questions. Realize the customer's desire to move away from *pain* and/or towards *pleasure* and the *pull* or motivation to make that picture a reality. Without a detailed future picture the brain will fill in, often with inaccurate details. Once you have a shared future picture with your customers, you will both start to think of ways to achieve it.

# 7     The pull

## Reflection and benefit questions

In Chapter 6 we introduced you to the complete picture method. We emphasized the importance of developing a present and future picture by using observation and asking two types of question – that is, present and future questions.

If this has been insufficient to close the sale you have probably failed to create a strong enough pull. To remedy this, you can use two new types of question: reflection and benefit questions.

Reflection questions are designed to direct the customer's attention to the pain and propel them towards the pleasure. When this psychological pull between the 'present picture' and the 'future picture' is strong enough, the customer will decide to buy in order to move *away from pain* and *towards pleasure*.

Reflection questions, as their name implies, encourage the customer to reflect on the pain of the current situation. Examples are:

- 'How will you feel if you miss this year's holiday?'
- 'What effect will not meeting your budget have on your next year's allocation?'
- 'How will you cope next time the machine breaks down and you have no back-up?'

The benefit question encourages the customer to consider the pay-off achievable by moving from the present to the future picture. Benefit questions ask 'What will it mean to you?' and, as their name implies, encourage the customer to tell you the benefit! Once they have the benefit there's a natural increase in the pull. Examples of benefit questions are as follows:

- 'What will it mean to you to be able to take a holiday this year?'
- 'What effect will being 10 per cent ahead of budget have on the following year's allocation?'
- 'What will it mean to you the next time your machine breaks down and you have an immediate back-up to take over?'

Now that you know what benefit your customers are seeking you can show how your product or service offers that specific benefit or you can walk away and waste no more of your and their time, knowing that you cannot help them at present.

In the space below, make up some reflection and benefit questions you could ask for your own product and/or service.

**Reflection questions** are designed to direct the customer's attention to the pain and propel him or her towards the pleasure.

1 _____

2 _____

3 _____

4 _____

5 _____

**Benefit questions** are any questions that help build up the 'future picture' containing pleasure.

1 _____

2 _____

3 _____

4 _____

5 _____

# Long and short cycles

Every contact with a client is an activity. In short-cycle selling the prospect might buy on the strength of one sales presentation. This is a one-activity sale and is mainly found in retail selling, impulse purchases or for items purchased over the telephone.

A long-cycle sale takes two or more presentations. This could be for such things as the purchase of heavy industrial equipment, a home, a computer system or hiring a consultant. Here the sales process covers a series of activities over an extended period. Activities could comprise a proposal, follow-up telephone calls, seeking additional information, a visit to on-site employees to gather data or running a focus group. Each of these counts as an activity.

# Memory rhythms

For long-cycle sales the challenge lies in deciding when to follow up. On the one hand you do not want to be forgotten by the prospect but, on the other, you don't want to be regarded as a nuisance. If you are to be remembered by the prospect you need to understand their memory rhythms, as illustrated in Figure 7.1.

The diagram shows how quickly we tend to forget information. You will see that the drop in the 'amount recalled' – the vertical axis – is rapid and dramatic without follow-up in 10 minutes, 24 hours, one week and one month (the horizontal axis). This means you need to review the main points of your presentation at the end of the conversation and then find ways to remind your prospect of your presentation within one day, seven days and, finally, one month. Think of what you can send to fit into these time slots – follow-up letters, telephone calls, literature and so on. Use your creative imagination and write the times in your diary so that you *remember*!

Each activity you create in a long-cycle sale is just one more step towards a sale. If the activity does not achieve the desired sales outcome it will still have been beneficial as you will have learned new information that can be used to help you reach your objectives. Activities should never be considered as failures but simply as progressions towards the final sale.

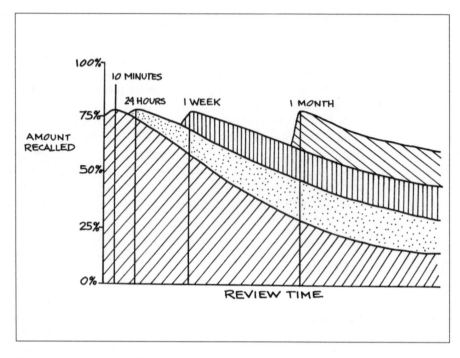

**Figure 7.1**   Memory rhythms

# Feedback

Feedback must be actively sought and encouraged. You must specify that you seek feedback which is honest, specific and as detailed as possible. Feedback should also be directly related to the sales goal. For example:

*Salesperson*: Mrs Smith, you said that if you do not reach your sales target, you would have a serious problem with your executive team. You also mentioned that you have a budget for advertising and have had good results with our magazine before. Please tell me why we cannot agree on a new contract.'

*Prospect*: 'You're right, I know your magazine pulls. However, your increase in advertising rates is too large for me to justify.'

Feedback is not a one-way street. You must be prepared to give it as well as receive it.

*Prospect*: 'I just cannot see the point of this long-term health policy, I've never been sick.'
*Prospect*: 'You don't seem to understand. This is too much for me to spend right now.'
*Prospect*: 'No, I don't want to be loaded with more monthly payments.'

Without feedback, you can only assume that the path you are following will lead to your sales goal. This carries the risk of filling in the blanks with nothing more than suppositions and hypotheses.

Feedback is the lifeline to sales success. It tells us about the effectiveness of the activities we've chosen to undertake in order to achieve our sales goals. It also provides us with the appropriate action plan towards future adjustments that may be necessary in order for us to become successful in selling.

# Closing the sale

You have established the 'present picture' and the pain. You have developed a 'future picture' of away from pain and towards pleasure. You have, through a series of activities in a long-cycle sale, established the pull. In a short-cycle sale this may have only taken one activity or contact. You are now in a position to close the sale.

Provided you have achieved sufficient pull, the sale should close itself! You need to ask a closing question and take some action to show the customer that the deal is completed.

We described various closing techniques in *Brain Sell*. The most common closure is to simply ask a question with a built-in alternative: 'When can we deliver this, Miss Thomas, Wednesday or Friday?' The customer will consider this question. Even though the silence may seem to last forever, do not start talking, because, if you do, you will distract the customer's thought process – which is the last thing you want to do.

Although there are numerous books on the subject of closing the sale, our advice is to ask a simple closing question and wait for the response. If the customer is not convinced, then you need to accept that feedback and start creating more pull with reflection and benefit questions.

Once the customer agrees to buy, take some type of action – fill in paperwork, obtain a deposit, do anything that will register with the prospect, via their senses, that the sale has been completed.

# Reinforcing the decision

Our brains want to protect us at all times and make the best decisions. This survival instinct is important when you close the sale. Now is the time to reassure your customer that they have made a wise decision. A simple comment such as 'You will have years of pleasure from this ...' is all that is needed. In other words, reinforce the future picture – the benefits and *pleasure* or the absence of *pain*!

# Summary

In this chapter we discussed the importance of the pull. Reflection and benefit questions can strengthen the pull. Sales are either long- or short-cycle in duration. In a long-cycle sale – one that involves several activities over a period of time – consider the customer's memory rhythms to decide when to follow up. Finally, we covered the importance of feedback and that closing question. Always end the sales conversation by reassuring the customer that they have made a wise decision.

# PART THREE

## The Sales Genius Diary

The 12 Sales Genius Traits – Observations
The 12 Sales Intelligences – Activities

# Introduction

Diaries are a way of recording progress, daily observations, successes, obstacles to be overcome and feedback for learning purposes. Interestingly, geniuses throughout time have kept detailed diaries.

## The Sales Intelligences Master Progress Sheet

On the following page you will find the Sales Intelligence Master Progress Sheet. The vertical axis covers the 12 Sales Intelligences that make up a Sales Genius. The horizontal axis comprises a time line with five separate occasions to score your progress. Study this page before proceeding.

Now complete the Sales Genius Intelligences Master Progress Sheet as follows.

Under the column 'Date – 1st' enter today's date and, for each of the 12 Sales Intelligences, rate yourself on a scale from 0 to 100, 0 being non-existent and 100 being perfect. Then add up your total score and enter in the appropriate box on the 'Total score' line.

## THE SALES INTELLIGENCES MASTER PROGRESS SHEET

| Dates | | Your score (0 = non-existent 100 = perfect) | | | | |
|---|---|---|---|---|---|---|
| | | 1st | 2nd | 3rd | 4th | 5th |
| 1 | Sensory | | | | | |
| 2 | Intuitive | | | | | |
| 3 | Logical | | | | | |
| 4 | Verbal | | | | | |
| 5 | Spatial | | | | | |
| 6 | Personal | | | | | |
| 7 | Musical | | | | | |
| 8 | Mind-body | | | | | |
| 9 | People | | | | | |
| 10 | Technical | | | | | |
| 11 | Visual | | | | | |
| 12 | Creative | | | | | |
| | **Total score** | | | | | |

### Dates

You will notice that there are spaces left for four scores. These will be done at different intervals during the 100-day diary that follows. These scoring dates will be:

- 1st – day 1
- 2nd – day 25
- 3rd – day 50
- 4th – day 75
- 5th – day 100

On each of these dates you will find a Progress Sheet. Complete the score on the respective sheet and then transfer the score to the corresponding column on this Master Progress Sheet. This will allow you to keep track of your progress on one page, but *not* be influenced by your previous score!

This benchmarking of your progress is important. On a day-to-day basis it's difficult to assess your progress. However, over a period of 100 days, you will be able to see the progress you have made under dates on p. 80.

# Activities for the 12 Sales Intelligences

For each of the 100 days there is a different activity that relates to the 12 Sales Intelligences covered in Chapter 4. As you do these activities, you may well ask yourself 'How does this relate to selling?', for it will not always be obvious. However, by developing these different Sales Intelligences, you are developing all your abilities, including your ability to sell. Remember when you did your art masterpiece, following the Conni Gordon Four-Step Method in Chapter 4, we explained that, by increasing your creative intelligence, you improve all intelligences. The same rule applies as you work through the 100 activities. So do not be concerned about the relevance to selling, simply complete the activities day-by-day.

Some activities will take more than a day to complete, as they are ongoing, while others involve learning new skills, so be patient, playful and persistent.

# Observations of the 12 Sales Genius traits

It is generally accepted that if you wish to acquire a new habit, characteristic or trait it takes 30 days of conscious practice. The Sales Genius Diary is constructed so that some of the 12 traits of the Sales Genius discussed in Chapter 2 appear on each of the diary pages (starting on p. 189) so that you can write down your daily observations with respect to the individual traits. The diary pages are at the end of this book. The first 33 days concentrate on the first four traits – peak sales vision, planning to sell, persistence and learning from mistakes.

We recommend that, at the end of each day, you complete your observations for all four traits. You will be surprised at the amount of detail you will discover, especially as the weeks go by. You will remember from studying our graph on memory rhythms in Chapter 7 that if you do not reinforce the material you want to learn within 24 hours, there is a dramatic fall-off. Now you know how the brain works, you understand how important it is to complete this diary every 24 hours in order to master the materials.

Once you reach Day 34, the next four traits appear on your daily diary pages – belief in self, company, products and service, being an expert, commitment and desire to succeed.

Some space is still allotted for the first four traits, which you still need to complete, but the main emphasis will be on the new four.

On Day 67 the final four traits are introduced – mastermind group, truth and honesty, imagination and energy. The first eight traits will still be present, but with limited space for completing observations. However, the main focus will be on the last four traits. As previously mentioned, it takes about 30 days of consistent practice to change habits. There are no short-cuts and, in some cases, it might take up to six weeks of consistent practice. That is why we stress the importance of completing the daily observations if you wish to incorporate the Sales Genius formula into your life and reap the rewards.

## THE SALES GENIUS TRAITS MASTER PROGRESS SHEET

| Dates | | Day 1 | Day 33 | Day 66 | Day 100 |
|---|---|---|---|---|---|
| 1 | Peak Sales Vision | | | | |
| 2 | Planning | | | | |
| 3 | Persistence | | | | |
| 4 | Learning from mistakes | | | | |
| 5 | Belief in self, company, products/service | | | | |
| 6 | Expertise | | | | |
| 7 | Commitment | | | | |
| 8 | Desire | | | | |
| 9 | Mastermind Group | | | | |
| 10 | Truth and honesty | | | | |
| 11 | Imagination | | | | |
| 12 | Energy | | | | |
| | **Total score** | | | | |

# Differences

It is very important to notice any small improvement which occurs. Regularly ask yourself, 'What's different now from when I started?' Spend time observing and reviewing your efforts and think about how your sales career might have been without these changes. Appreciate your progress. Accept compliments from customers and associates as your sales improve and your sales career takes off. Observe how much more enjoyable life becomes when you have a peak sales vision and create positive solutions to reach it. Notice how excuses for failure disappear, how you stop losing your focus and accepting incorrect information and how your brain will support you in learning new and interesting things.

# Summary

The Sales Genius Diary will help you develop your Sales Genius in a scientific, time-proven manner. Each day follows an activity developing one of the 12 Sales Intelligences: on the relevant diary page record your observations on the respective 12 Sales Genius traits on which you are working.

# Activity 1: Squelchers

As you work through your daily activities, you might hear a little voice inside your head making some of the following statements. We call them 'squelchers', because they attempt to sabotage your efforts!

- 'I've been there, done that.'
- 'This is more than my job's worth.'
- 'I've tried this before.'
- 'I don't have time for this.'
- 'Where will I find resources for all this?'
- 'This is too complicated.'
- 'This is a stupid idea.'
- 'I can't do that.'
- 'I've heard some crazy ideas, but this beats them all.'
- 'I'm too old to do this now.'
- 'I'm happy with the way things are.'
- 'If it ain't broke, don't fix it.'
- 'I don't have the expertise for this.'
- 'My customers won't appreciate this.'
- 'I'm already overextended.'
- 'It's not going to be any better.'
- 'No one communicates with me.'
- 'Why doesn't my boss read this first?'

*Now add your own.*

Put a tick next to the squelchers you have heard yourself say. Usually the acknowledgement alone will make them disappear. If you still are having trouble with them, Activities 2 and 3 provide additional plans of attack.

# Activity 2: Clean up

Squelchers can be removed using the 3As – Awareness, Analysis and Action.

- **Awareness**. Catch yourself squelching. It's a form of whining, blaming, complaining and commiserating.
- **Analysis**. Once you are aware of the destructive thoughts, analyse them for what they are and even have some fun with them. If you continue to whine, blame and so on it becomes a little boring! Turn it into a game. Whine out loud. If you are with others, play 'This is the worst day of my life...'. Exaggerate and take turns.
- **Action**. Now that you are aware of your squelchers and have analysed the part of you that loves to squelch, you have the power to choose a more constructive response. Here are some ideas:
  - 'Let me find a way to work on this.'
  - 'I'll plan time to do this programme daily.'
  - 'I am choosing how to respond.'
  - 'What do I need to do to improve...?'
  - 'I am taking total responsibility for my actions.'
  - 'How can I use my creative brain to solve this?'

# Activity 3: Positive mind

If you think negatively, you will fail; if you think realistically and positively, you will succeed. Negative thought patterns create a mental and physical resistance that hinders performance. To start accustomizing your brain to focus on the positive do the following activity, with the help of a friend.

Try this experiment. Hold your arm out straight, while your friend tries to push it down. As you resist the pressure say out loud 'I love my job', over and over again. Now change the phrase to 'I hate my job' and compare the strength you experience. Notice how much stronger you are and how much better your performance is when you say 'I love... – a positive thought pattern.

Changing thoughts to 'I love...' instead of 'I hate...' will result in a much better sales performance.

Now make a list of everything you hate and turn them into 'I love' statements. See how it changes both your focus and your sales career.

I hate _____

I hate _____

I hate _____

I hate _____

I hate _____

I hate _____

I hate _____

I hate _____

I hate _____

I hate _____

I hate _____

# Activity 4: Change that voice

Improve your memory by improving your inner voice.

Develop the ability to read, hearing the writer's voice, even if you invent the voice. This will help you understand more of what you are reading and will make remembering any material you wish to recall far easier!

Imagine the following situations and hear them in the appropriate voice:

1   Your favourite customer talking to a friend about your ability to sell.
2   One of your managers describing a new product or service.
3   One of your closest friends telling you what a great potential you have in sales.
4   One of your schoolteachers, describing a competitor's product or service.
5   One of your favourite television or radio announcers talking about current market conditions.

# Activity 5:  Backwards and forwards

The following exercise will speed up your mental ability to work with numbers.

1   Count silently from 1 to 50 as fast as you can.
2   Count out loud from 1 to 50 as fast as you can.
3   Count silently backwards from 50 to 1.
4   Count out loud backwards from 50 to 1 as fast as you can.
5   Recite the alphabet silently as fast as you can.
6   Recite the alphabet silently backwards as fast as you can.
7   Count silently from 50 to 100 as fast as you can.
8   Count out loud from 50 to 100 as fast as you can.
9   Count silently backwards from 100 to 50.
10   Count out loud backwards from 100 to 50 as fast as you can.

# Activity 6: Double-hand doodles

This exercise will help you develop your spatial intelligence, while activating your whole creative brain. It's an excellent activity to do first thing in the morning! You will need some paper (use the space below for your first practice) and two pens or pencils.

Hold a pen or pencil in each hand. Next, create a picture with both hands simultaneously – that is, the left hand does exactly what the right does. Study the example.

LEFT HAND

RIGHT HAND

# Activity 7:  Successful ideas

 Think of an idea to solve a sales problem that you have been considering for some time. Use the following five-step approach to help clarify your thinking.

**Step One**: Write down your idea.

**Step Two**: Answer the following two questions:
A.    What's right with the idea?

B.    What's wrong with the idea?

**Step Three**: Does the idea fulfil your outcome – that is, does it do what you want it to do? If your answer is 'yes', how? (If 'No', rethink Step One!)

**Step Four**: Is the idea an improvement on what already exists? If so, how?

**Step Five**: Is the time right for implementing this idea? If not, when should you implement it?

# Activity 8: Commonality

 Search for commonality amongst the following pairs of items. For example: 'What do an elephant and a banana have in common?' Answer: a thick skin, live in the same climate and so on.

1   What do IBM and Disney World have in common?

2   What do coffee and Laplanders have in common?

3   What do shoelaces and trains have in common?

4   What do a mountain and chocolate have in common?

5   What do walking and talking have in common?

# Activity 9: Take a break

Take short brain breaks during work periods. This allows time to integrate the materials you have been working with and also helps reduce stress.
Appropriate brain breaks result in more productive work. You can:

- Go for a walk.
- Listen to music.
- Do some stretching exercises.
- Daydream.
- Make up your own brain break activities.

_____

_____

_____

_____

_____

_____

Now tick those you intend to do!

# Activity 10: Lace up

 Take two minutes to list how many uses there are for a shoelace in the box below.

| **A shoelace** |
| --- |
|  |

You can do this exercise to develop your creative intelligence, any time with any object. A paperclip, a toothbrush, a pencil, a match ... make up your own!

# Activity 11: Together again

Find any old broken electrical appliance, such as a toaster, radio, hairdryer or clock, that you no longer intend to use.

Next, with the appropriate tools, break the item down into as many different components as possible. Make certain that you are aware of how each piece is designed to fit with the others and keep all the pieces in one place.

Now put the appliance back together. Consider how the designer made the appliance work in the first place and how each piece fits into the whole design.

# Activity 12: Guided missile

Complete the following sequence. Find one item *within your view* beginning with each letter listed below. **Do not skip letters. Proceed to the next letter only after completing the one with which you are working –** in other words, do not move on to 'C' before 'A'.

This activity can be done repeatedly in different locations.

A _____    N _____

C _____    P _____

E _____    R _____

G _____    T _____

I _____    V _____

K _____    X _____

M _____    Z _____

# Activity 13: Makes sense

A critical sales skill is that of being able to see more than other people. By developing your salesenses you will achieve that! This activity can be carried out anywhere at any time. Simply vary the colours and shapes, and always do it for one minute.

As you practise this activity on different occasions keep a record of your answers.

Spend one minute seeing how many objects in the room are green.

| Number of objects | Date |
| --- | --- |
| _____ | _____ |
| _____ | _____ |
| _____ | _____ |
| _____ | _____ |
| _____ | _____ |

Spend one minute seeing how many objects in the room contain triangles.

| Number of objects | Date |
| --- | --- |
| _____ | _____ |
| _____ | _____ |
| _____ | _____ |
| _____ | _____ |
| _____ | _____ |

# Activity 14:  Round the clock

Your brain is working 24 hours a day. Think of it as a giant reference library that you can't always fully access during your waking hours. Books are being taken off the shelves and read, as new books (experiences) are constantly arriving. While you sleep, the librarians are busy at work, refilling, sorting and opening new files for all that new information (including insights and connections). It's during this time that your librarians can find much of that information you have been searching for!

If you have a question or problem you're having difficulty in solving, consciously pose that question to yourself at bedtime. You may often discover that in the morning or some time during the next few days, the answer comes to you. Take time each morning to capture your overnight ideas and solutions by writing them down.

Tonight before retiring, place in your mind a sales situation/problem you want to solve. Draw a picture, image or symbol of the sales situation/problem in the centre of the box below. Tomorrow morning on awakening, record and/or Mind Map the solutions. Keep this page, with some coloured pens, next to your bed. Practise daily!

Keep blank paper and a pen by your bed to capture great ideas when they occur!

# Activity 15:  Turn off the TV

It is tempting to return home from a tiring day and relax in front of the TV. However, your sales brain will benefit far more from reading, be it books, magazines, newsletters or trade publications. Reading needs more concentration and uses more of your mental skills.

Reading nourishes your sales brain. It's also good for your 24-hour sales brain to be consolidating and making new associations with what you have been 'reading' during the night while you sleep (see Activity 14).

This is a simple new habit you need to acquire. Once you have read in the evenings 30 minutes for 30 consecutive days you will have developed the new reading habit. Read a wide range of materials from science to fiction to classics – you will find this far more rewarding than watching TV and your sales knowledge base will expand considerably. Furthermore, you will find that, because of all this new knowledge, many more ideas on how to increase your sales will pop into your conscious mind.

# Activity 16: Play games

Remember all those games you played at school? Monopoly, chess, snap, battleships and many, many more. Yet how many of those games do you play today? Mental games are excellent for developing your sales brain because they work on all the cortical skills.

Take every opportunity to play games either with children or with an interested partner. Chess and bridge clubs abound in every country. Make a list of all the different games you could play. Then start playing them!

**Games I could play:**

1 _____

2 _____

3 _____

4 _____

5 _____

6 _____

7 _____

8 _____

9 _____

10 _____

Why don't you become involved in the Mind Sports Olympiad and see a wide range of games from around the world? (See Resources at the end of this book for contact details.)

# Activity 17: Think of a song

Music and rhythm help you remember. Conduct the following activity to prove this point to yourself. In the space below write out the words of a song you know well, without the melody in mind. Stop when you first stumble.

Now try it again, this time with the melody in mind. See if you can go further!

**Song title:** _____

**Words, no music:** _____

_____

_____

**Words with music:** _____

_____

_____

# Activity 18: Thermometer

To develop intuitive intelligence you need to tune into your intuitive self.
Learn to tune into your clients and/or prospects by using the thermometer technique. Below list the names of six customers. Above each name is a thermometer with a scale marked from 1 to 10 (10 being the best you can possibly feel towards the client or prospect and 1 being the worst). Now take a deep breath, relax and decide where you would mark the thermometer for each name. Let your intuitive self guide you.

|  |  |  |
|---|---|---|
| 10 | 10 | 10 |
| 9 | 9 | 9 |
| 8 | 8 | 8 |
| 7 | 7 | 7 |
| 6 | 6 | 6 |
| 5 | 5 | 5 |
| 4 | 4 | 4 |
| 3 | 3 | 3 |
| 2 | 2 | 2 |
| 1 | 1 | 1 |
| CLIENT _____ | CLIENT _____ | CLIENT _____ |

|  |  |  |
|---|---|---|
| 10 | 10 | 10 |
| 9 | 9 | 9 |
| 8 | 8 | 8 |
| 7 | 7 | 7 |
| 6 | 6 | 6 |
| 5 | 5 | 5 |
| 4 | 4 | 4 |
| 3 | 3 | 3 |
| 2 | 2 | 2 |
| 1 | 1 | 1 |
| CLIENT _____ | CLIENT _____ | CLIENT _____ |

# Activity 19: Creative thinking

Thinking through association uses the whole creative brain. It can have a step-by-step approach.

For example, when I think of the word 'chocolate', I make the following associations:

CHOCOLATE ⇨ DELICIOUS ⇨ FAT ⇨ UNHEALTHY ⇨ EXERCISE

As you can see, 'CHOCOLATE' reminds me of 'DELICIOUS', reminds me of 'FAT', reminds me of 'UNHEALTHY', reminds me of 'EXERCISE'.

Try this for yourself. Start with the word 'INVESTMENT'.

_____ ⇨ _____ ⇨ _____ ⇨ _____

How did you do? What are the implications of associative thinking when it comes to communicating with your customer?

# Activity 20:  Finding new customers

Having completed Activity 19, 'Creative Thinking', you may have noticed that each association leads to another. Here is a sales example of selling to groups:

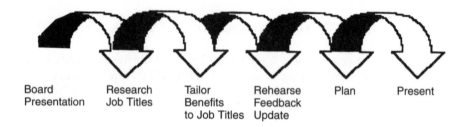

| Board<br>Presentation | Research<br>Job Titles | Tailor<br>Benefits<br>to Job Titles | Rehearse<br>Feedback<br>Update | Plan | Present |

Taking the phrase 'Finding new customers' as a starting point, write down what comes to mind as you Think-Link.

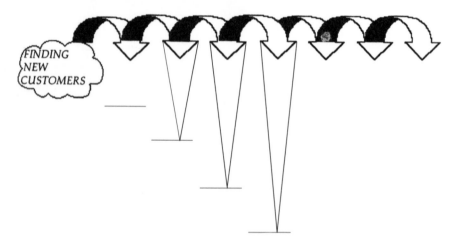

# Activity 21: Make me feel good

 An important people skill is to make other people feel good – whether it is good about you, buying from you, making a purchase or dealing with your company. Yet how often do we pay any conscious attention to this skill? Take time to complete the following activity by listing how many ways you can think of to make customers feel good.

**I can make a customer feel good by:**

1 _____

2 _____

3 _____

4 _____

5 _____

6 _____

7 _____

8 _____

9 _____

10 _____

11 _____

12 _____

13 _____

14 _____

15 _____

# Activity 22: Creative insights

It's important to develop mental alertness in creating thoughts, ideas and text. This activity will develop your creativity and focus as well as improve your powers of recall.

Use the following list of words, and within two minutes, arrange all the words in any order, along with other words, to create a story. Keep to the time-limit of two minutes.

| customer | address | pen | magazine |
|----------|---------|-----|----------|
| sherry | pond | music | orange |
| chemistry | silver | sunny | penny |

**My story**

# Activity 23: A mouthful

Here are five ways to improve your creative speech. Select one.

1 Build your vocabulary. Learn new words daily.
2 Mind Map speeches and practise them on friends, and or audio/video tape them.
3 Analyse your speech against the Brain Sell Grid (page 37).
4 Volunteer for speaking tasks at your office or with any public speaking group.
5 Listen to great speakers and analyse what makes them superior.

**Keep a record of your progress.**

**Decide on a plan of action:**

**Record your progress:**

# Activity 24:  Alignment check

The first circle below is divided into eight segments. One segment is labelled 'work', another 'health', another 'relationships', another 'exercise' and another 'expertise'. The final three are up to you (ideas are diet, adventure, fun, spirituality, rest, hobbies). Place a dot in each segment at the degree to which you are fulfilled in that area (the outer rim indicates high fulfilment; the inner circle indicates low fulfilment). Connect the dots. This will show you where you need to exert extra effort to obtain a balanced lifestyle. Use the second circle for future review and for comparison purposes.

**Example:**

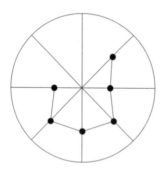

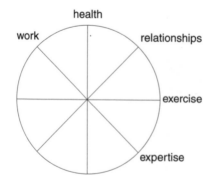

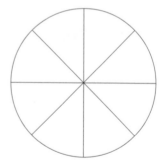

# Activity 25: Air head

 You need a physical exercise programme to develop aerobic capacity, strength and flexibility, including *aerobic activity* sustained for a minimum period of 20 minutes, at least three times a week. Good aerobic activities include jogging, swimming and cycling. Such activities will yield many benefits. They strengthen your cardiovascular system, and improve blood and oxygen flow to your mind and body. Your brain is less than 3 per cent of your body weight but uses up to 30 per cent of the body's oxygen. Being aerobically fit increases your capacity to process oxygen with the result that you will enjoy reduced fatigue, improved alertness and emotional stability. It also improves digestion and regulates weight. However, always check with your doctor before embarking on any exercise programme.

**Decide on a plan of action**     **Record your progress**

1 _____    _____
2 _____    _____
3 _____    _____
4 _____    _____
5 _____    _____
6 _____    _____
7 _____    _____
8 _____    _____
9 _____    _____
10 _____    _____
11 _____    _____
12 _____    _____
13 _____    _____
14 _____    _____
15 _____    _____
16 _____    _____
17 _____    _____
18 _____    _____
19 _____    _____
20 _____    _____
21 _____    _____

## THE SALES INTELLIGENCES MASTER PROGRESS SHEET

| Dates | | Your score (0 = non-existent 100 = perfect) | | | | |
|---|---|---|---|---|---|---|
| | | 1st | 2nd | 3rd | 4th | 5th |
| 1 | Sensory | | | | | |
| 2 | Intuitive | | | | | |
| 3 | Logical | | | | | |
| 4 | Verbal | | | | | |
| 5 | Spatial | | | | | |
| 6 | Personal | | | | | |
| 7 | Musical | | | | | |
| 8 | Mind-body | | | | | |
| 9 | People | | | | | |
| 10 | Technical | | | | | |
| 11 | Visual | | | | | |
| 12 | Creative | | | | | |
| | **Total score** | | | | | |

Once you have scored your 12 Sales Intelligences transfer them to the Master Progress Sheet on page 80 in the appropriate column and record the date.

# Activity 26: Spaced out

Here are five ways to improve your spatial skills:

1 Mind Map the news, films or telephone conversations.
2 Solve crossword puzzles.
3 Play games such as chess and Monopoly.
4 Take up any type of dancing.
5 Go for walks and estimate the distance between you and objects ahead (for example, trees). Then check your accuracy by walking to them.

**Keep a record of your progress.**

| Decide on a plan of action | Record your progress |
|---|---|
| 1 | |
| 2 | |
| 3 | |
| 4 | |
| 5 | |
| 6 | |
| 7 | |
| 8 | |
| 9 | |
| 10 | |
| 11 | |
| 12 | |
| 13 | |
| 14 | |
| 15 | |

# Activity 27: Reconnect

There are so many people you have met but rarely get in touch with. Think of all those business cards hidden away and names in your address book that you have overlooked for ages! Yet all contacts form your network for future sales!

What could you do to reconnect with them? Send a postcard, gift or calendar? Make a telephone call? Once you decide what is appropriate, take action. Note down the names and the method you will use to re-establish contact below.

| | Name | Contact method | Outcome |
|---|---|---|---|
| 1 | | | |
| 2 | | | |
| 3 | | | |
| 4 | | | |
| 5 | | | |
| 6 | | | |
| 7 | | | |
| 8 | | | |
| 9 | | | |
| 10 | | | |
| 11 | | | |
| 12 | | | |
| 13 | | | |
| 14 | | | |
| 15 | | | |

# Activity 28: Mirror talk

This activity has been used by such leaders as Winston Churchill and Theodore Roosevelt. Look into a mirror when you are alone and speak to yourself with enthusiasm about your sales career and how you are planning to succeed.

You may feel a little foolish at first. That's only natural, but it will soon give way to a more confident and powerful you!

**Keep a record of your progress.**

|  | Practice date | Progress |
|---|---|---|
| 1 | _____ | _____ |
| | | _____ |
| 2 | _____ | _____ |
| | | _____ |
| 3 | _____ | _____ |
| | | _____ |
| 4 | _____ | _____ |
| | | _____ |
| 5 | _____ | _____ |
| | | _____ |
| 6 | _____ | _____ |
| | | _____ |
| 7 | _____ | _____ |
| | | _____ |
| 8 | _____ | _____ |
| | | _____ |
| 9 | _____ | _____ |
| | | _____ |
| 10 | _____ | _____ |
| | | _____ |

# Activity 29: Retreat

Take some time to be by yourself – ideally a day or two – and go somewhere you like and where you won't be interrupted. Do the things you like to do. It could be walking, swimming, reading a book or simply doing nothing. Perhaps you want to daydream, sleep or meditate, or think things over. Build in some play time for yourself – something creative, such as painting, drawing, singing, dancing or simply writing whatever comes to mind. This is precious time, time you have earned, and time you can spend getting to know yourself. It is also time to reflect on your values, goals and progress that you have made.

**Decide now when and where this will take place and write or Mind Map it in the space below as a commitment to yourself.**

# Activity 30:  YES!

To create an instant positive state of mind for excellent sales performance, you can use an anchor as a reference point or a cue. Here you are linking a relaxed body with an alert mind, resulting in a calm, focused state of being.

To do this, think back to a time when you did something really well. Create an inner model of excellence. What did you see? What did you hear? What did you feel? When you feel that you are actually reliving that situation fully, clenching your dominant hand, thrust it upward and release your energy, uttering the word 'YES'. Whenever your state of mind needs a boost, repeat this activity.

**Mind Map or write below the multisensory memory of *your* success.**

# Activity 31: Object analysis

Object analysis is the creative process of making objects give us answers to our sales problems. Sometimes the insights for solving our problems lie right under our noses and below our conscious mind. Here's what to do. Select an object. It does not matter what it is. Whatever you select is fine. Allow your intuitive mind to come into play. Look closely at the selected object and then identify its various attributes (for example, table = support, service, elegance, shapely and so on).

Allow the attributes to trigger off associations in your mind. Don't be too literal; play with words, their sounds, colours, meanings and nuances. You will be able to create endless insights and associations. Keep a record below.

**Object selected:** _____

| Attributes of object | Insights through association |
|---|---|
| _____ | _____ |
| _____ | _____ |
| _____ | _____ |
| _____ | _____ |
| _____ | _____ |
| _____ | _____ |
| _____ | _____ |
| _____ | _____ |
| _____ | _____ |

# Activity 32: Singing

 Singing is one of the most therapeutic activities for both the mind and the body. It allows you to extend vocal sounds in a way that speaking does not. Consider how singing has been incorporated into religious ceremonies throughout the ages! Singing exercises the larynx, vocal cords and feedback areas to the brain that receive music and voice. Decide now on songs you can sing, and when you will sing them – for example, in the shower, in the car, in a choir, to the kids. Then start practising for a few minutes, daily for the next few weeks. You will soon notice an improvement in the quality of your speaking voice.

**Make a note of your intended repertoire of songs and when and where to sing them.**

|  | Songs to sing | When and where to sing them |
|---|---|---|
| 1 | | |
| 2 | | |
| 3 | | |
| 4 | | |
| 5 | | |
| 6 | | |
| 7 | | |
| 8 | | |
| 9 | | |
| 10 | | |

# Activity 33:  Eyes closed

 To help develop your senses, stand some distance from a blank wall. Make certain that there is no furniture between you and the wall.

Now, with your eyes closed and your arms extended, inch your way slowly towards the wall. Do not open your eyes until you believe your hands are about an inch from the wall. Now open your eyes. How close were you?

If you do touch the wall while your eyes are closed, repeat the activity from the beginning.

**Record your observations in the space below for future reference.**

# Activity 34: Completion

Review unsuccessful sales experiences that are still bothering you. With hindsight what would you have done differently? What lessons can you learn for another time?

Then thank the experience for its lesson, wrap it up (mentally) and move on.

**Unsuccessful sales experiences**

1 _____

2 _____

3 _____

4 _____

5 _____

**Lessons learned**

1 _____

2 _____

3 _____

4 _____

5 _____

# Activity 35: Reinvent yourself

Picture the type of sales professional you want to be. Cultivate in yourself the qualities you seek by doing whatever it takes to develop them – for example, through classes, coaching, therapy, deportment, speech therapy, diet, exercise and so on.

**List your desired qualities below. Then develop them.**

| | Desired qualities | How I will develop them |
|---|---|---|
| 1 | | |
| 2 | | |
| 3 | | |
| 4 | | |
| 5 | | |
| 6 | | |
| 7 | | |
| 8 | | |
| 9 | | |
| 10 | | |

# Activity 36: Clean up the soundtrack

This activity allows you to deal with your inner conflicting voices that are sabotaging your relationships with your prospects, customers, peers and managers. It involves taking time alone to converse with yourself about those past fears, worries or hurts.

Simply hold a conversation between yourself and whatever or whoever is bothering you, using your imagination to create the responses made by the opposing party. Carry on with these conversations, remembering that all these conflicts are resolvable.

You may wish to record yourself, to listen to what you have to say!

# Activity 37: Diet

Good diet improves circulatory and immune systems, prevents injury and optimizes your enjoyment of movement.

To live a balanced life eat a balanced diet. Eat fresh, wholesome and aesthetically pleasing foods. Have fresh fruit, vegetables and fibre daily. Drink a minimum of eight glasses of water daily and moderate your intake of salt, sugar, fat, red meat, caffeine and alcohol. Use all your senses to enjoy your food. Maintain a healthy, normal weight so that you have ample energy for daily tasks, a better appearance, increased alertness and improved self-esteem.

Monitor your 'normal' diet for five days. Notice which foods/drinks are taken in excess or are lacking. Note them below and plan to cut them back or increase them. Note the improvements.

| | Food/drink | Cut back (✔) | Increase (✔) | Improvement |
|---|---|---|---|---|
| 1 | | | | |
| 2 | | | | |
| 3 | | | | |
| 4 | | | | |
| 5 | | | | |
| 6 | | | | |
| 7 | | | | |
| 8 | | | | |
| 9 | | | | |
| 10 | | | | |

# Activity 38: Sales story

 Think of your most recent successful sale and outline or Mind Map it below in a logical sequence of events.

Next tell a friend, associate or family member about that sale.

Tell the story in a clear logical way and paint word pictures as you recount it. This activity helps you build up a strong inner model of what sales success is to you, making it easier to duplicate in future.

# Activity 39:  The year 2010

Write down below how you consider technology will be supporting your sales effort by the year 2010. For example, think how you would have answered this question in 1985 when there were no mass-produced computers and fax machines, mobile phones, pagers and e-mail had not been invented!

By projecting from the past, in logical steps to the future, you are developing technical intelligence and discovering ways in which modern technology can help you improve your sales. (You may even notice a great new idea!)

**My vision for the role of technology in supporting sales is:**

# Activity 40: Amnesia

 A quick way to increase sales is to remove any resentment you may be harbouring towards anyone – customers, past and present managers, colleagues, suppliers, family members and ex-friends! Why? Because resentment ties up and blocks the mental and emotional energy that you need daily for your sales career. Imagine, for a moment, that you have amnesia and have forgotten all those old hurts! Here's how.

Find some quiet time when you won't be interrupted. Write a letter to the person towards whom you are feeling any resentment, anger or hostility. Put down everything that comes to mind, from the extremes of all your hurt to all your forgiveness. Take your time. When you have finished you have some choices. Send it, burn it, or file it away. You might want to call the person concerned and talk on the telephone or arrange a meeting. It's up to you. Repeat this process with each person you are holding any anger or resentment against. Then notice the difference between how you are currently feeling and how you felt in the past.

**List below the people against whom you are harbouring anger or resentment.**

| Person | Action taken | |
|---|---|---|
| *Example* | | |
| Fred | Letter written ✓ | burned ✓ |
| Gill | Mind Map ✓ | phone |
| 1 _____ | _____ | |
| 2 _____ | _____ | |
| 3 _____ | _____ | |
| 4 _____ | _____ | |
| 5 _____ | _____ | |
| 6 _____ | _____ | |
| 7 _____ | _____ | |
| 8 _____ | _____ | |
| 9 _____ | _____ | |
| 10 _____ | _____ | |
| 11 _____ | _____ | |
| 12 _____ | _____ | |
| 13 _____ | _____ | |

# Activity 41: People watch

To develop your people skills and ability to read people, you need to study how people interact, their body language, facial expressions and gestures. Is there a series of behaviours that you can learn to identify from a smile and handshake to a farewell?

For the next week spend 15 minutes a day observing how people interact in public. Find a suitable place to stand – a shopping precinct, cinema, street corner – and develop your people-watching skills.

Keep a record of your observations on this page for future reference. Look for the following body language and write down what you think is going on.

### People-watching observations

Eye contact:

Physical closeness:

Mimicking each other's actions:

Touching:

Facial expressions:

Emotions:

# Activity 42: Increased sales!

Think up as many ways as you can to increase your sales by 1 per cent over your previous month's sales, and list them in the space below.
**Ways:**

Think up as many ways as you can to increase your sales by 10 per cent over your previous month's sales, and list them in the space below.
**Ways:**

Think up as many ways as you can to increase your sales by 100 per cent over your previous month's sales, and list them in the space below.
**Ways:**

Think up as many ways as you can to increase your sales by 1000 per cent over your previous month's sales, and list them in the space below.
**Ways:**

See how it is just as easy to create ideas to increase by 1000 per cent as it is for 1 per cent!

Now do them!

# Activity 43: Focus that picture

Concentration can be improved by focusing daily on an object. Take your watch, for example. Look at the face of your watch and concentrate on the second hand or digital seconds. For the next minute think only of the seconds, repeating silently the word 'one'. Should any distracting thought enter your mind (such as 'how many sales have I made today?') move on to the number 'two', while still watching the seconds pass.

If, for example, you had 12 extraneous thoughts during the one minute, at the end of that time you would have been repeating to yourself the word 'twelve'. When you have completed the exercise, make a note of the number you reached in your observation space below. In this way you will have a record of the date and score as you progress!

The goal is to be still repeating the word 'one' at the end of the minute. Once you can do this, repeat this exercise with increasing degrees of difficulty: for example, watching the seconds without saying anything to yourself, while humming a tune or in a noisy room.

**Date**                     **Number of extraneous thoughts**

_____          _____

_____          _____

_____          _____

_____          _____

_____          _____

_____          _____

_____          _____

_____          _____

# Activity 44: The room

 Think of an office, at home or at work, or one in which you have worked. With your eyes closed mentally remove each piece of furniture from the room. In your mind's eye, picture the room bare. Next mentally paint the walls in a new colour or design. Then mentally replace all the furniture in new positions and with a completely new look.

Practise this activity several times and count the number of items you originally removed.

# Activity 45: Sales commercial

Prepare a 45-second radio commercial for yourself. That's you selling you! Plan what you will say. Write or Mind Map out a brief outline in the space below. Now stand in front of a mirror and practise delivering your commercial. Commit it to memory and then practise again without any memory aids.

**Outline of commercial:**

# Activity 46: Tone-up

During the course of a busy day you need to tone up your mind–body connection. This reduces stress as well as increases mental alertness.

In a sitting or standing position, close your eyes and begin to rock backwards and forwards, very slowly and gently. Ignore your breathing and any distracting noises around you and concentrate only on the rocking movement of your body.

Gradually allow the rocking movement to become smaller and smaller, until it's so imperceptible that a person standing next to you would barely notice the motion. Continue with this gentle motion. Should your mind wander, simply bring it back to the rocking motion.

This activity can be done any time, anywhere and, in a minute or two, will tone up your mind–body connection.

# Activity 47: Remember that customer

This activity will take a week and will require additional notepaper. Make a conscious effort to remember each customer you speak to each day. If your conversation is held over the telephone, think of their name, voice and any personal details they have given you. If you speak to them face-to-face, remember their name, information obtained, their personal appearance – hair colour, eyes, face and body features. Then, each night, write down or Mind Map as much as you can about each person. Describe them, name them and record what they each said.

# Activity 48: Musical secrets

Music can often open the doors to the subconscious mind, revealing many perceptive ideas and answers to pressing problems. Describe in detail below a current problem that you are facing and to which you need answers. It might concern, for example, how to increase sales, launch a new product or enter a new market.

Next put the pen and paper aside, make yourself comfortable and remain silent, breathing deeply, for a few minutes. Then play a piece of your favourite music. Listen to the music. Do not think of the problem. Simply listen to the music. You may well notice solutions and/or answers creeping into your mind. When the music stops, write down the insights you received.

**Current problem:** _____

_____

**Musical choice:** _____

**Solutions:** _____

_____

_____

_____

_____

_____

_____

_____

_____

# Activity 49: Circle of support

You can obtain many sales leads from your social support network. This activity will help you discover that group.

Place your name in the innermost circle below. In the first ring around your name, list all your 'intimate' friends and associates – people you would turn to in a time of need. In the next circle list friends whom you see regularly but who are not intimate friends. In the next circle list people you know, but only on a casual basis. Now that you have given structure to your social support network, think how you can communicate with your circle of support and tell them what you are currently doing.

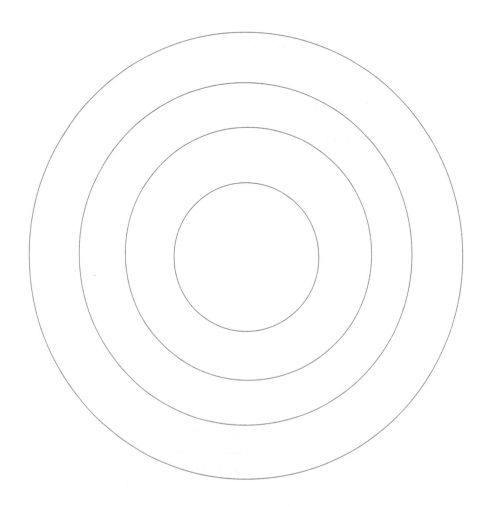

# Activity 50: Pressured or relaxed

In our daily life, situations constantly arise which can cause two psychological responses – being pressured or relaxed. The pressured response is the one that feels stressful both in mind and body: you are quick to judge, feel frustrated and take things personally. This is not the best frame of mind for building a sales career. However, in the relaxed mode, you are in a relaxed state of mind and body. You see the big picture, take things less personally, are flexible and calm and at your best. For the next few days become aware of which mode you are operating in.

**Note your personal observations below.**

| | MODE | RESPONSE |
|---|---|---|
| **Day 1:** | | |
| **Day 2:** | | |
| **Day 3:** | | |
| **Day 4:** | | |
| **Day 5:** | | |
| **Day 6:** | | |

## THE SALES INTELLIGENCES MASTER PROGRESS SHEET

| Dates | | Your score (0 = non-existent 100 = perfect) | | | | |
|---|---|---|---|---|---|---|
| | | 1st | 2nd | 3rd | 4th | 5th |
| 1 | Sensory | | | | | |
| 2 | Intuitive | | | | | |
| 3 | Logical | | | | | |
| 4 | Verbal | | | | | |
| 5 | Spatial | | | | | |
| 6 | Personal | | | | | |
| 7 | Musical | | | | | |
| 8 | Mind-body | | | | | |
| 9 | People | | | | | |
| 10 | Technical | | | | | |
| 11 | Visual | | | | | |
| 12 | Creative | | | | | |
| | **Total score** | | | | | |

Once you have scored your 12 Sales Intelligences transfer them to the Master Progress Sheet on page 80 in the appropriate column and record the date.

# Activity 51: Hidden beliefs

Do you have hidden beliefs that are holding you back? These hidden beliefs are often found in our subconscious mind, and this activity allows you to contact them! You may find this an extremely insightful activity which can be repeated many times.

In the left-hand column below you will see a prepared statement. Read the statement and then in the 'Response' column write down *whatever thoughts come to mind*, entering layer after layer of responses. If you discover an inhibiting belief, stop and plan an action around it. You can repeat this activity, entering any statement you wish in the left-hand column and repeating the process.

| Statement | Response |
|---|---|
| My sales are increasing every day. | |
| I am networking more and more. | |
| Customers are recommending me. | |

# Activity 52: Accomplishments

Think of something you have done that you are really proud of. Next think what you did to achieve this one outstanding accomplishment. What were the qualities or characteristics that you displayed? Was it persistence or patience for example? List below as many of these qualities or characteristics as you can.

1 _____

2 _____

3 _____

4 _____

5 _____

6 _____

7 _____

8 _____

9 _____

10 _____

Review these characteristics from time to time. Remember you still can use all of them in your current sales efforts.

# Activity 53: Sales analysis

Think about two or three of your most rewarding sales experiences. What made them so memorable?

In the space below write or Mind Map the elements of these experiences, using the following questions as a guide.

- Were you working with your hands? With numbers? With words? With concepts? With people?
- Were you helping people in any way?
- Were these successes the result of a long period of working towards success?
- How would you apply these lessons to your present sales activities?

**My most rewarding sales experiences**

# Activity 54: Change agent

 Think back to the most important changes you have made in your life.

Now recall some of the negative things that you thought would happen as a result of the change. How many of these negative things actually did happen?

What conclusions can you reach from this review?

**Record or Mind Map your conclusions below.**

# Activity 55: Learning something new

 Think of a new skill you would like to learn (for example, using a computer or learning a foreign language). What resources would you need? Where would you go to learn this skill? Set yourself a plan of action and then do it!

**New skill:**

| Resources needed | Plan of action |
|---|---|
|  |  |

# Activity 56: Sound sense

As you read the following statements, imagine different people making these statements and hear the statement in their voice. This activity helps develop your salesenses.

- 'Yes!'
- 'I'll buy it.'
- 'Hi!'
- 'I appreciate...'
- 'Watch out!'
- 'How much?'
- 'My pleasure.'
- 'What did you expect?'
- 'That was great!'
- 'When I was your age...'
- 'You're terrific.'
- 'Thank you.'

# Activity 57: Watch the time

 Look at your watch and observe the time. Now, with your eyes closed, and not counting, sit still for what you judge to be three minutes. Look at your watch again and check to see how accurate you were.

Do this exercise whenever you have a spare three minutes, such as when you are waiting for an appointment, bus, train or plane. It will help you develop your sense of time. A good sense of time will result in your being on time for appointments, and accurately assessing how much time you have left in a sales presentation or sales meeting!

Also, guess the time before looking at your watch. See how often you are correct (or close)!

**Note your observations below.**

# Activity 58: Someone new

Each day for the next seven days speak to someone you have never spoken to before. It could be anybody, anywhere. Ask them questions about themselves and see how much information you are able to obtain. You will need to share something about yourself, of course, but the stranger should do most of the talking.

**Record your progress below.**

Day 1: _____

_____

Day 2: _____

_____

Day 3: _____

_____

Day 4: _____

_____

Day 5: _____

_____

Day 6: _____

_____

Day 7: _____

_____

# Activity 59: Wish list

This activity is designed to make you proactive rather than reactive to the opportunities that daily present themselves to you. Starting today, and adding to the following list over the next week, write down everything you wish to accomplish for the rest of your life. It could be climbing Kilimanjaro or being the number one salesperson in your company. Write them all down in the space below, as you think them up over the next week. Then watch for opportunities to turn them into reality and make happy memories!

| | |
|---|---|
| 1 _____ | 20 _____ |
| 2 _____ | 21 _____ |
| 3 _____ | 22 _____ |
| 4 _____ | 23 _____ |
| 5 _____ | 24 _____ |
| 6 _____ | 25 _____ |
| 7 _____ | 26 _____ |
| 8 _____ | 27 _____ |
| 9 _____ | 28 _____ |
| 10 _____ | 29 _____ |
| 11 _____ | 30 _____ |
| 12 _____ | 31 _____ |
| 13 _____ | 32 _____ |
| 14 _____ | 33 _____ |
| 15 _____ | 34 _____ |
| 16 _____ | 35 _____ |
| 17 _____ | 36 _____ |
| 18 _____ | 37 _____ |
| 19 _____ | 38 _____ |

# Activity 60: Computer games

Buy or borrow a computer game which appeals to you and play it. All computer games are designed to improve your spatial skills by shifting your brain from analytical thought to spatial thought. Keep increasing the level of difficulty as you become more proficient. Chess is an excellent game to play on the computer. If you do not own a computer, maybe you can play on a friend's computer, or visit a computer showroom, arcade or cybercafe.

**Make notes on your computer game progress below.**

# Activity 61:  Picture maths

Much of the mathematics for price discounts and quotations can be performed by picturing the numbers in your head. This takes a little practice but will enhance your ability to work with numbers.

Here are some activities to help you start this new technique:

1   Picture the numbers 1 to 20.
2   Picture the multiplication table 12, from 1 times 12 to 12 times 12.
3   Picture your home telephone number.
4   Picture the amount of money you have in a bank or savings account.
5   Picture 511 minus 400 and the answer.
6   Picture the numbers 1 to 12 on the face on a clock.
7   Picture the current temperature in degrees centigrade or fahrenheit.
8   Picture the number of days in the current month.
9   Picture 773 plus 412 and the answer.
10  Picture the numbers from 50 to 35 backwards – that is 49, 48 and so on.
11  Picture the numbers 175 minus 36 and the answer.

# Activity 62: Relax

What makes you relax? What are your favourite activities for unwinding and restoring your sense of balance? List below everything you can think of. Revisit this list and add to it as more ideas occur.

1 _____

2 _____

3 _____

4 _____

5 _____

6 _____

7 _____

8 _____

9 _____

10 _____

11 _____

12 _____

13 _____

14 _____

15 _____

# Activity 63: Changing shape

To develop your technical intelligence, think through the construction of everyday appliances and machines and how they work. A novel and effective way to do this is as follows. If you don't know how the following items work, then just make it up!

1   Imagine you are a piece of paper and you are about to go through a copying machine. With your eyes closed, imagine in as much detail as possible the process you would experience.
2   Imagine you are the petrol in a car engine and are about to go through the engine's motor, turning yourself into the explosive power that drives the engine. With your eyes closed, imagine in as much detail as possible the process you would experience.
3   Imagine you are a television signal being beamed from a local TV station. With your eyes closed, imagine in as much detail as possible the journey you would go through to become a picture on a television screen.
4   Imagine you become your voice and are travelling through your telephone, via satellite, into a friend's telephone on the other side of the world. With your eyes closed, imagine in as much detail as possible the journey you would make.

# Activity 64:  Map it

This activity develops your spatial intelligence. Think of the route you take to work, whether by car, bus, walking or train. If you are working from home, then use a route you take to visit a client or a friend. Next, as you mentally travel this route, turn it into a mental map. Now imagine that you are in a helicopter looking down and then draw the route in your mind.

Next, using the box below, draw it from start to finish, with all the details you can – landmarks, changes in terrain and compass directions. When you have finished, compare it to an actual map of the area!

# Activity 65: Musical memory

This activity will help develop your musical memory, which will enhance your general powers of recall.

Sit in a relaxed posture, with your eyes closed, and take a few deep breaths. Have a friend read the following list to you, with a 20-second pause between each word. As you hear the word, produce the appropriate sounds in your mind's ear.

1  A thunderstorm.
2  Car traffic.
3  Waves hitting the shore.
4  A dog barking.
5  Your favourite song.
6  A sports crowd roaring.
7  A violin playing.
8  Bells ringing.
9  A choir singing.
10  Yourself singing an original song.

# Activity 66: The letter

Select a business journal or trade publication. Find an item of interest or hot topic. In the space below, write a letter to the editor expressing your point of view on this topic. Decide whether or not to send this letter. Revise this letter twice, with the intention of improving it each time. Think of your language and the response it will produce in the reader.

---

**Letter to the editor**

_____

_____

_____

_____

_____

_____

_____

_____

_____

_____

_____

_____

_____

_____

# Activity 67: Mastermind group

One of the characteristics of a Sales Genius is forming, developing and using a mastermind support group. List the members of your mastermind group, comprising from three to seven people. Explain to them what you are doing and arrange a time and place when you can contact them. Contact might mean a telephone call, an after-work drink or a meal together.

### My mastermind group

| Name | Contact by | Contact when |
|------|-----------|-------------|
| *For example:* | | |
| *Mary Roman* | *Lunch* | *Monthly* |
| 1 _____ | _____ | _____ |
| 2 _____ | _____ | _____ |
| 3 _____ | _____ | _____ |
| 4 _____ | _____ | _____ |
| 5 _____ | _____ | _____ |
| 6 _____ | _____ | _____ |
| 7 _____ | _____ | _____ |

# Activity 68: Colours

Visualize the colour green. Start by visualizing the door to your home as green. Now think of a car that is entirely green. This could be your own or a friend's car. Make the green car so large that it fills your complete mental screen. Next make the car a dark green, a light green and a fluorescent green.

Change the colour of the car to red, blue, orange, pink, white and finally back to the original green.

Imagine driving this car and looking out of the window. What colours would the other cars be? The buildings? The streets?

**Note below any observations about this activity.**

# Activity 69: Smell success

Concentrate on the following smells, and describe them as best you can either out loud or in writing.

1 Coffee.

2 Newspaper.

3 Soap.

4 Fresh linen.

5 Flowers.

6 Fresh baked bread.

7 Hot tar.

8 Unused rooms.

9 New pencils.

10 Singed feathers.

# Activity 70: Change pace

Try this activity during the next week, when you find yourself handling a difficult sale in which you know there are significant obstacles to overcome, or when you are about to face a difficult client. Stop what you are doing and take a five-minute walk. Do not think of the sales situation you have left behind. Simply enjoy the walk.

When you return, tackle the problem again. This time write or draw or Mind Map the solution and, if possible, play some music and see what you come up with!

**Record your progress below.**

# Activity 71: Area of influence

To develop your people skills and ability to network with new prospects you need to expand your area of influence. One good way to do this is to connect with new people through group activities. This could be as varied as joining a club, attending school parent meetings, volunteering for a local charity work, or joining an investment group, reading group and so on.

Think of a group or groups you would like to join, then decide when you will do it. The rest is up to you!

| Group(s) I will join | When |
| --- | --- |
| _____ | _____ |
| _____ | _____ |
| _____ | _____ |
| _____ | _____ |
| _____ | _____ |
| _____ | _____ |
| _____ | _____ |
| _____ | _____ |
| _____ | _____ |
| _____ | _____ |
| _____ | _____ |

# Activity 72: Picture it!

For this activity you need some uninterrupted time and to be seated comfortably.

- Take a few deep breaths and relax.
- Picture all the people you have spoken with today.
- What did they look like?
- What was the colour of their hair and their eyes?
- What were their ages and their heights?
- What clothes were they wearing?
- Did they have any particular mannerisms?
- How did they walk and hold themselves?

Now picture the customers you have seen in the last few days, with as many details from above as possible. Then picture your favourite customer with as many details from above as possible, and draw below.

# Activity 73: Values

Our values are the foundations of our belief systems, our self-worth and our daily behaviours.

First, study this list.

| Values | Column 1 | Column 2 |
|---|---|---|
| Meaningful work | | |
| Security | | |
| Love | | |
| Family | | |
| Friendship | | |
| Competition | | |
| Status | | |
| Personal growth | | |
| Health | | |
| Community service | | |
| Adventure | | |
| World peace | | |
| Spirituality | | |
| Making a difference | | |
| Peace of mind | | |
| Wealth | | |
| Cooperation | | |
| Power | | |
| Happiness | | |
| Integrity | | |
| Recognition | | |
| Patriotism | | |
| Respect | | |
| Loyalty | | |
| Independence | | |
| Wisdom | | |
| Teamwork | | |
| Leisure | | |
| Variety | | |

**Exercise 1**

In column 1, rate your 'top ten' values with 1 being highest.

**Exercise 2**

Now that you have established what you believe are your 'top 10' values, this exercise will display the day-to-day reality of your value system.

In column 2, with 1 being the highest, rate the 'top 10' values according to how you spend your time.

When reviewing the differences between column 1 and column 2, you will see a snapshot of what you can create. You may find you have a dilemma between what you value most and how you spend your time. It is important to act on the values that you personally rate highly to achieve a greater sense of harmony for yourself and your family.

# Activity 74: Concentration power

Here is an activity for developing your ability to concentrate, which is so important in selling and for improving memory.

Slowly draw a pencil across a plain piece of paper. Direct your attention to the point where the pencil point becomes the line. Each time your mind wanders, draw a kink in the line. When you have completed a line, double back. How long can you keep an unbroken line of awareness? Count the number of kinks you make and note it in the space below as a record of your progress.

Repeat this activity daily until you are able to draw a continuous line without any kinks.

**Example**

| Date: | | | | | | | | |
|---|---|---|---|---|---|---|---|---|
| **Number of kinks:** | | | | | | | | |

# Activity 75:  Your musical muscle

To develop your musical intelligence, you need a plan of action. Here are a series of ideas you can use, plus space for your own. Decide which ones are best for you and write next to them the action you intend to take to:

| Ideas | Actions |
|---|---|
| 1   attend concerts | _____ |
| 2   learn to play a musical instrument | _____ |
| 3   join a folk group or choir | _____ |
| 4   read letters or newspaper aloud for 10 minutes a day in a sing-song voice | _____ |
| 5   make a list of all the background music you hear in one day | _____ |
| 6   join a musical appreciation group | |
| 7   explore a different kind of music | _____ |
| 8   review all your records, tapes and CDs and play them | _____ |
| 9   make notes on how music influences our daily lives | _____ |
| 10  read about the lives of the great musicians. | _____ |

## THE SALES INTELLIGENCES MASTER PROGRESS SHEET

| Dates | | Your score (0 = non-existent 100 = perfect) | | | | |
|---|---|---|---|---|---|---|
| | | 1st | 2nd | 3rd | 4th | 5th |
| 1 | Sensory | | | | | |
| 2 | Intuitive | | | | | |
| 3 | Logical | | | | | |
| 4 | Verbal | | | | | |
| 5 | Spatial | | | | | |
| 6 | Personal | | | | | |
| 7 | Musical | | | | | |
| 8 | Mind-body | | | | | |
| 9 | People | | | | | |
| 10 | Technical | | | | | |
| 11 | Visual | | | | | |
| 12 | Creative | | | | | |
| | **Total score** | | | | | |

Once you have scored your 12 Sales Intelligences transfer them to the Master Progress Sheet on page 80 in the appropriate column and record the date.

# Activity 76: Creative preparation

To be creative, to come up with new ideas, you need to give your brain as much stimulation and background information on the topic being considered as possible. This way, your brain makes new associations, resulting in fresh creative ideas. If you want new ideas on how to increase sales you need to do your homework first. This means reading books and articles on the subject, attending lectures and speaking to salespeople who have achieved higher sales.

Decide on the area in which you wish to have creative insights. Next, note or Mind Map everything you can do to obtain the necessary background information. Finally, place an action date next to each item and start taking action!

**Area of creative interest:** _____

| Background information | Action date |
| --- | --- |
| _____ | _____ |
| _____ | _____ |
| _____ | _____ |
| _____ | _____ |
| _____ | _____ |
| _____ | _____ |
| _____ | _____ |
| _____ | _____ |
| _____ | _____ |

**or Mind Map:**

# Activity 77: Living words

Now that you have experienced developing your different senses, you can strengthen the way in which you access and recall information.

Take a favourite business book, journal or magazine and find a descriptive passage involving a person or people. Next, read this passage slowly and place yourself there as one of the main characters in the text. See, hear, smell, taste and touch everything you read as if you were living this role in real life. This might take a little practice but it is well worth the effort and will do wonders for your memory and recall.

**Keep a record of your progress and observations below.**

# Activity 78: Spatial scanning

 Spatial scanning is important for many daily sales activities such as locating and perceiving objects in space, and observing clients. Scan the following letters and cross out all the Ps in the next 30 seconds! You can repeat this exercise with any written material and any letter!

```
Q E C P S E O L K M E S E F R C Y B G W S X U P E R T
W X R C W C E H Y Z I N P E R V Y B M W X P U T C D
W Z X W J E C P V E S U N R C Y P D R B S W S R C W J
R C S T H J P O L W F N E A S Y N E D X Y L W P M R Y
Q A W S C W V E B E T H E N W X Y K H I P L M W S O
W S P O L Y N R D P E F S W Z A H E R C E S B E S I P B
W S E D W C R F B W X Y N E A T G P O L R B E S C T V E
W A S W C B W N Y V M K L P R D P E C W S C R C P L D
Y V E P L Y V E S X R V E U N R O L S P L E C E X W X R
W S C E W S B R P P L M T B R C E S H E C X J U I T E W E
```

# Activity 79: Be Dale Carnegie

In Dale Carnegie's classic book on people skills *How to Win Friends and Influence People* he details masterful ways of doing just that.

Imagine that you are Dale Carnegie and, without referring to the book, list seven key points on how to win friends and influence people that you would advise your readers to use.

**How to win friends and influence people**

1 _____

2 _____

3 _____

4 _____

5 _____

6 _____

7 _____

Now apply these to your own daily contact with all the people you meet!

# Activity 80: Force fit

Obtain an article on any technical topic falling outside your area of expertise. Read it, then make notes, copy diagrams or anything else that you find interesting. Then write down a sales problem you are presently facing. Now see how the information you have just read suggests new solutions to your sales problem.

Force fit them together and you will be surprised at some of your insights.

**Technical notes:**

**Sales problems:**

**New solutions:**

# Activity 81: Favourite character

 Imagine that you are a character in your favourite film or novel.

Next, taking a scene from that film or from one of the chapters in the novel, imagine what is happening around you.

Spend the next few minutes describing out loud all that is happening. Repeat the activity whenever you have the opportunity and make notes on your progress below. This develops your ability to imagine, explain and create a multisensory story around a topic.

**Favourite character:**

**Notes:**

Notice how, over time, your ability to visualize and then achieve successful sales outcomes improves!

# Activity 82: Seeking

 A good way to build your sales business is to seek new customers. There are dozens of sources from which you can discover new prospects, from telephone books to the Internet.

Think of as many different sources as you can and list them below. You will find this an interesting activity to do with an associate. Once you have your list, start using it!

1 _____

2 _____

3 _____

4 _____

5 _____

6 _____

7 _____

8 _____

9 _____

10 _____

11 _____

12 _____

13 _____

14 _____

15 _____

# Activity 83: Visualize

What follows is a series of activities designed to improve your visual intelligence.

1   Visualize four things that make you feel happy.
2   Visualize four of your favourite foods.
3   Visualize four types of transport.
4   Visualize four objects/items that begin with the letter 'T'.
5   Visualize four of your relatives.
6   Visualize four of your favourite cities.
7   Visualize four of your favourite films.
8   Visualize four of your favourite animals.

Practise these during waiting periods or when taking a break.

# Activity 84: Make it up!

Creativity has much to do with 'just making it up' or adding something new to what already exists. This activity develops that skill.

**Make as many different things out of the circles and squares as possible. Study the examples.**

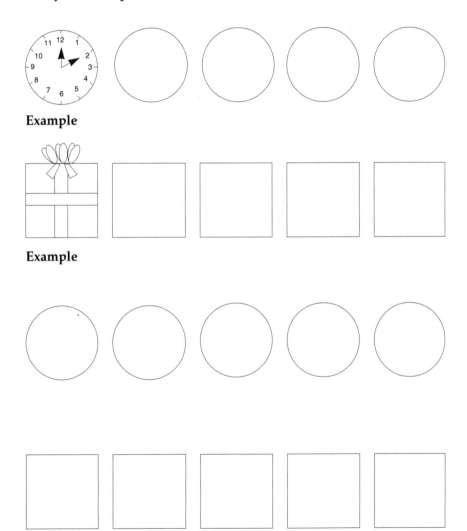

Example

Example

# Activity 85: Refocus

When you are feeling stressed, such as before an important sales appointment or critical telephone call, you need to relax and regain your focus to be at your best. This activity fulfils that purpose.

Close your eyes, breathe in and exhale slowly. Now shift your breath to your abdomen and take ten slow, complete relaxed breaths. First, fill your abdomen and then chest with air. As you breathe out, chest first, then abdomen, silently say 'ten-relax'. On the second exhalation, say 'nine-relax'. Count down to one. Should you lose the count, pick it up where you were.

**Keep a record of your progress and observations below.**

**Notes:**

_____

_____

_____

_____

**Mind Map:**

# Activity 86: Big picture listening

Are you a good listener? Improving your listening skills not only enhances your people skills but will certainly improve your selling. One of the main problems with listening is failing to accurately hear what is said and formulating your response before you have received the complete message!

You can overcome this classical listening trap by forming a picture in your mind of what you are hearing. Not only does this stop you from jumping in with your response but it helps you recall what has been said. Furthermore, if there are gaps in your picture – that is, incomplete data – it enables you to ask questions to complete the picture.

For the next seven days listen to at least two people a day, using this technique. Only respond to each person when you have the complete picture. Keep a list of names of those with whom you have used this technique. Refer back to these names and see their respective 'pictures' for weeks and months afterwards!

| Day | Name | Name |
|-----|------|------|
| 1 | | |
| 2 | | |
| 3 | | |
| 4 | | |
| 5 | | |
| 6 | | |
| 7 | | |
| 8 | | |
| 9 | | |
| 10 | | |

# Activity 87: Ten things to do

Here are ten activities to improve your verbal intelligence. Select three that you are not currently engaged in.

1  Join a book club and read, read, read.
2  Read a quality newspaper daily, for a wealth of information and new ideas.
3  Learn one new word a day and use it in your sales conversations.
4  As you speak to customers, pay particular attention to the words they use. Can you match their vocabulary – that is, use similar words to them?
5  Learn to use a word processor and practise writing 100-word articles about any aspect of your sales career.
6  Make up your own jokes, write them down and refine them.
7  Attend a workshop on speed reading.
8  Join a speakers' club. Toastmasters International meet all over the world on a regular basis.
9  Learn processes to improve your memory.
10 Revisit your personal library and read the books you have not yet read or completed. Set yourself a deadline by which to finish reading these books.

Select one of these activities to work on at a time and then proceed through the list.

| Activity | Date |
|----------|------|
|          |      |
|          |      |
|          |      |
|          |      |
|          |      |
|          |      |
|          |      |
|          |      |

# Activity 88:  Association

When you are searching for a solution to a problem, use the following process. Find a comfortable seat and sit upright with your spine erect. Take a few relaxing breaths until you feel at ease. Look around the room and, in the appropriate spaces below, write down the following:

- the first item that attracts your attention (*item 1*)
- any item in the room that you do not like (*item 2*)
- any item you can see in the room that you would like to receive as a gift (*item 3*).

Then read the instructions that follow.

**Item 1:**
**Connection:**


**Item 2:**
**Connection:**


**Item 3:**
**Connection:**


Now take item 1 and consider how it could offer a solution to the problem you are working on. Write down that solution (however strange it might seem) under 'Connection' following item 1.

For item 2, make the connection between the item and the problem. Think of what you should avoid doing to solve the problem. Write your answer under 'Connection' following item 2.

Finally, for item 3, make the connection between the item selected and the problem and then a connection with someone who can help you with this problem. Write the name under 'Connection' following item 3.

# Activity 89: Taste sense

Chocolate is a delicious subject for most of us when developing our senses. Think of as many kinds of chocolate as you can – for example, hot chocolate in a blue china cup, black forest gateau, chocolate milk.

Once you have listed the different chocolates, what are your corresponding memories? Where were you when you experienced each type?

| Types of chocolate | Memories |
| --- | --- |
| 1 _____ | _____ |
| 2 _____ | _____ |
| 3 _____ | _____ |
| 4 _____ | _____ |
| 5 _____ | _____ |
| 6 _____ | _____ |
| 7 _____ | _____ |
| 8 _____ | _____ |
| 9 _____ | _____ |
| 10 _____ | _____ |
| 11 _____ | _____ |
| 12 _____ | _____ |
| 13 _____ | _____ |
| 14 _____ | _____ |
| 15 _____ | _____ |

# Activity 90:  Best place and time

To be creative you need to be prepared and disciplined. Prepared means having a pen or pencil and paper at hand all the time. You never know when you may receive that next fleeting creative breakthrough. Being disciplined means preparing your mind to be creative at certain times. Even though creative thoughts can come at any time, you can stimulate your best time. You are influenced by your biological rhythm – the time of day or night when you are at your best. Do you know when this is? Are you aware of the types of situation in which you often receive your best ideas? Is it walking in the park, taking a shower, driving in traffic? This preparation is crucial to high creativity.

**Write or Mind Map your best times and best places for creative ideas.**

My best place is:                                  My best time is:

Now that you have identified these elements, place yourself in them whenever you need a creative boost.

# Activity 91: Excellent communicators

You have been asked to make a presentation at work on the subject of 'What makes an excellent communicator?'

The presentation is to be given in three weeks' time, so you have time to research the subject. A one-page handout is required, consisting of the seven main headings of your speech.

In preparing the handout, note or Mind Map below what you consider to be the seven most important features of an excellent communicator.

**Excellent communicators are:**

1   _____

2   _____

3   _____

4   _____

5   _____

6   _____

7   _____

Now ask yourself how many of these qualities you possess. How can you enhance those you have and obtain those you lack? Make notes below.

# Activity 92: Sales success

 See yourself as a sales success. First read through these instructions. Then, with your eyes closed, form a clear mental image of yourself as a sales success. Imagine that you can adjust your mental image in the same way as you can adjust a television picture by turning the different dials.

First select the sharpness dial. Make your picture as clear as possible with all the details – can you see every detail of your clothing? Next, make your picture bright. Turn up the brightness until you sparkle! Now, adjust the size. First make the picture smaller, then larger and, finally, the correct size. How about the colour? Make certain that you adjust the colours to be exactly right – neither too bright nor too dull. Finally, play with the sound. Turn up the volume so you can clearly hear everything surrounding you and then adjust it to the correct volume.

**Keep a record of your observations below.**

# Activity 93: Association buzz

To create new ideas you need to start making those associations in your head buzz. This activity is bound to achieve the association buzz and can be carried out at any time, with any letter!

Take the letter T, and in the next three minutes list as many words as you can starting with T. It's always a good idea if you can compete with a partner when conducting this exercise.

T _____     T _____
T _____     T _____
T _____     T _____
T _____     T _____
T _____     T _____
T _____     T _____
T _____     T _____
T _____     T _____
T _____     T _____
T _____     T _____
T _____     T _____
T _____     T _____
T _____     T _____
T _____     T _____
T _____     T _____
T _____     T _____
T _____     T _____
T _____     T _____
T _____     T _____
T _____     T _____
T _____     T _____
T _____     T _____
T _____     T _____
T _____     T _____
T _____     T _____
T _____     T _____
T _____     T _____
T _____     T _____
T _____     T _____
T _____     T _____
T _____     T _____

# Activity 94:  Money builder

There is a direct correlation between your vocabulary and your income. The more words you know and use, the higher your income! So you can immediately start to earn more simply by learning one new word a day and using it in your daily conversations and in your correspondence! Why not carry with you a separate small notebook for your new words, so that you can review them frequently as you add more!

Another good strategy is to regularly play games such as Scrabble or Upward. Not only will you increase your vocabulary but you will also have fun with your family!

**Learn one new word a day.**

| | Word | Meaning |
|---|---|---|
| 1 | | |
| 2 | | |
| 3 | | |
| 4 | | |
| 5 | | |
| 6 | | |
| 7 | | |
| 8 | | |
| 9 | | |
| 10 | | |
| 11 | | |
| 12 | | |
| 13 | | |
| 14 | | |
| 15 | | |
| 16 | | |
| 17 | | |
| 18 | | |
| 19 | | |
| 20 | | |
| 21 | | |
| 22 | | |
| 23 | | |
| 24 | | |
| 25 | | |

# Activity 95: Computers are a must

More and more advertised positions state: 'Must be computer literate'. Computer skills are a must!

Learning to use a computer is excellent for your sales brain. You have to coordinate the hand and eye, follow directions and react quickly. There are numerous games you can play with your computer, including chess and card games. In the sales context, you can keep records, information, notes on meetings, price lists, client profiles – the list is endless. While you are on the road, you could use e-mail to communicate with head office, clients or even your family!

Knowledge of computers and their use is an important skill for today's salesperson. If you have not acquired such knowledge, don't delay any longer. Enrol in a training programme today. Your local college will run inexpensive courses. Pick up the telephone and enquire.

Write down below the steps you intend to take to become computer literate or to improve your computer literacy. If you are already computer literate, explore some new uses for applications and/or teach/help someone else.

1  _____

2  _____

3  _____

4  _____

5  _____

6  _____

7  _____

8  _____

9  _____

10 _____

# Activity 96:  Poetry

Find a book on poetry and open it at any page. Next, read the poem(s) on that page a few times, first rapidly, then slowly, then out loud and, finally, take your time to find new insights to some sales situations that you are currently facing.

**Write or Mind Map your insightful awarenesses or connections here.**

# Activity 97: Finger space

To improve your spatial intelligence, first read through, and then follow, the steps below:

- Standing erect, close your eyes and place your hands at your sides.
- Slowly bring the tips of your two index fingers together in front of you. Do this four times.
- Next, with your eyes still closed, touch the tip of your nose with your left index finger. Repeat with the index finger of your right hand and carry out both actions four times.

**Keep a record of your observations below.**

**Day 1:** _____

_____

**Day 2:** _____

_____

**Day 3:** _____

_____

**Day 4:** _____

_____

**Day 5:** _____

_____

**Day 6:** _____

_____

**Day 7:** _____

_____

# Activity 98:  Intuitive log

To develop your intuitive intelligence you need to stop approaching everything from a logical point of view or with an attitude that you have to be 'right'. Start tuning in to your intuitive self by noting small cues about your feelings. As time passes, you will have the opportunity to review these cues to ascertain whether they helped you in your daily sales situations.

Start by using the cues on this page and jotting down unexpected or odd feelings, thoughts or insights even though they are totally unrelated to the present work you are doing.

These messages can appear at any time and you simply note them in the space below, reviewing them every few days. For example, you might have a feeling that an old customer is attempting to contact you. On calling the customer, you discover that the customer had lost your telephone number and did indeed want to speak to you!

**Feelings:** _____

_____

_____

**Thoughts:** _____

_____

_____

**Insights:** _____

_____

_____

# Activity 99: Cooperation

To develop your people skills and customer base, you need to be able to cooperate with different types of people.

There are many ways you can cooperate in your daily working life – more than you are using now! Think up 15 new ways in which you can start cooperating – for example, listen more than speak, make eye contact and smile – and then decide to incorporate them into your behaviour. Do them!

**My 15 new ways to cooperate**

1 _____

2 _____

3 _____

4 _____

5 _____

6 _____

7 _____

8 _____

9 _____

10 _____

11 _____

12 _____

13 _____

14 _____

15 _____

# Activity 100:  Web page

You have been asked to design a web page to advertise yourself. In the space below, design the web page, taking into consideration the following:

1  Visitors to your web page should be offered a way to contact you.
2  Your web page should explain you in detail.
3  Your web page should be as attractive as possible.
4  Your web page should be brief and easy to read.

**Create the storyboard or Mind Map in the box below.**

## THE SALES INTELLIGENCES MASTER PROGRESS SHEET

| Dates | | Your score (0 = non-existent 100 = perfect) | | | | |
|---|---|---|---|---|---|---|
| | | 1st | 2nd | 3rd | 4th | 5th |
| 1 | Sensory | | | | | |
| 2 | Intuitive | | | | | |
| 3 | Logical | | | | | |
| 4 | Verbal | | | | | |
| 5 | Spatial | | | | | |
| 6 | Personal | | | | | |
| 7 | Musical | | | | | |
| 8 | Mind-body | | | | | |
| 9 | People | | | | | |
| 10 | Technical | | | | | |
| 11 | Visual | | | | | |
| 12 | Creative | | | | | |
| | **Total score** | | | | | |

Once you have scored your 12 Sales Intelligences transfer them to the Master Progress Sheet on page 80 in the appropriate column and record the date.

# Observation Diary

## The 12 Sales Genius Traits

| SALES GENIUS TRAITS | Day 1 | Day 2 |
|---|---|---|
| | Date: | Date: |
| 1.   Peak sales vision | | |
| 2.   Planning | | |
| 3.   Persistence | | |
| 4.   Learning from mistakes | | |
| 5.   Belief in self, company, product/service | | |
| 6.   Expertise | | |
| 7.   Commitment | | |
| 8.   Desire | | |
| 9.   Mastermind group | | |
| 10.  Truth and honesty | | |
| 11.  Imagination | | |
| 12.  Energy | | |

| Day 3 | Day 4 | Day 5 |
|---|---|---|
| Date: | Date: | Date: |
| | | |
| | | |
| | | |
| | | |
| | | |
| | | |
| | | |
| | | |
| | | |
| | | |
| | | |

| SALES GENIUS TRAITS | Day 6 | Day 7 |
|---|---|---|
| | Date: | Date: |
| 1.   Peak sales vision | | |
| 2.   Planning | | |
| 3.   Persistence | | |
| 4.   Learning from mistakes | | |
| 5.   Belief in self, company, product/service | | |
| 6.   Expertise | | |
| 7.   Commitment | | |
| 8.   Desire | | |
| 9.   Mastermind group | | |
| 10.   Truth and honesty | | |
| 11.   Imagination | | |
| 12.   Energy | | |

| Day 8 | Day 9 | Day 10 |
|---|---|---|
| Date: | Date: | Date: |
|  |  |  |
|  |  |  |
|  |  |  |
|  |  |  |
|  |  |  |
|  |  |  |
|  |  |  |
|  |  |  |
|  |  |  |
|  |  |  |
|  |  |  |

| SALES GENIUS TRAITS | Day 11 | Day 12 |
|---|---|---|
| | Date: | Date: |
| 1. Peak sales vision | | |
| 2. Planning | | |
| 3. Persistence | | |
| 4. Learning from mistakes | | |
| 5. Belief in self, company, product/service | | |
| 6. Expertise | | |
| 7. Commitment | | |
| 8. Desire | | |
| 9. Mastermind group | | |
| 10. Truth and honesty | | |
| 11. Imagination | | |
| 12. Energy | | |

| Day 13 | Day 14 | Day 15 |
|---|---|---|
| Date: | Date: | Date: |
| | | |
| | | |
| | | |
| | | |
| | | |
| | | |
| | | |
| | | |
| | | |
| | | |
| | | |

| SALES GENIUS TRAITS | Day 16 | Day 17 |
|---|---|---|
| | Date: | Date: |
| 1.  Peak sales vision | | |
| 2.  Planning | | |
| 3.  Persistence | | |
| 4.  Learning from mistakes | | |
| 5.  Belief in self, company, product/service | | |
| 6.  Expertise | | |
| 7.  Commitment | | |
| 8.  Desire | | |
| 9.  Mastermind group | | |
| 10.  Truth and honesty | | |
| 11.  Imagination | | |
| 12.  Energy | | |

| Day 18 | Day 19 | Day 20 |
|--------|--------|--------|
| Date: | Date: | Date: |
| | | |
| | | |
| | | |
| | | |
| | | |
| | | |
| | | |
| | | |
| | | |
| | | |
| | | |

| SALES GENIUS TRAITS | Day 21 | Day 22 |
|---|---|---|
| | Date: | Date: |
| 1.   Peak sales vision | | |
| 2.   Planning | | |
| 3.   Persistence | | |
| 4.   Learning from mistakes | | |
| 5.   Belief in self, company, product/service | | |
| 6.   Expertise | | |
| 7.   Commitment | | |
| 8.   Desire | | |
| 9.   Mastermind group | | |
| 10.  Truth and honesty | | |
| 11.  Imagination | | |
| 12.  Energy | | |

| Day 23 | Day 24 | Day 25 |
|--------|--------|--------|
| Date: | Date: | Date: |
| | | |
| | | |
| | | |
| | | |
| | | |
| | | |
| | | |
| | | |
| | | |
| | | |
| | | |

| SALES GENIUS TRAITS | Day 26 | Day 27 |
|---|---|---|
| | Date: | Date: |
| 1.   Peak sales vision | | |
| 2.   Planning | | |
| 3.   Persistence | | |
| 4.   Learning from mistakes | | |
| 5.   Belief in self, company, product/service | | |
| 6.   Expertise | | |
| 7.   Commitment | | |
| 8.   Desire | | |
| 9.   Mastermind group | | |
| 10.   Truth and honesty | | |
| 11.   Imagination | | |
| 12.   Energy | | |

| Day 28 | Day 29 | Day 30 |
|--------|--------|--------|
| Date: | Date: | Date: |
| | | |
| | | |
| | | |
| | | |
| | | |
| | | |
| | | |
| | | |
| | | |
| | | |
| | | |

| SALES GENIUS TRAITS | Day 31 | Day 32 |
|---|---|---|
| | Date: | Date: |
| 1. Peak sales vision | | |
| 2. Planning | | |
| 3. Persistence | | |
| 4. Learning from mistakes | | |
| 5. Belief in self, company, product/service | | |
| 6. Expertise | | |
| 7. Commitment | | |
| 8. Desire | | |
| 9. Mastermind group | | |
| 10. Truth and honesty | | |
| 11. Imagination | | |
| 12. Energy | | |

| Day 33 | Score |
|--------|-------|
| Date: | |
| | |
| | |
| | |
| | |
| | |
| | |
| | |
| | |
| | |
| | |
| | |

Place your scores on the Sales Genius Traits Master Progress Sheet on page 82.

| SALES GENIUS TRAITS | | Day 34 | Day 35 |
|---|---|---|---|
| | | Date: | Date: |
| 1. | Peak sales vision | | |
| 2. | Planning | | |
| 3. | Persistence | | |
| 4. | Learning from mistakes | | |
| 5. | Belief in self, company, product/service | | |
| 6. | Expertise | | |
| 7. | Commitment | | |
| 8. | Desire | | |
| 9. | Mastermind group | | |
| 10. | Truth and honesty | | |
| 11. | Imagination | | |
| 12. | Energy | | |

| Day 36 | Day 37 | Day 38 |
|---|---|---|
| Date: | Date: | Date: |
|  |  |  |
|  |  |  |
|  |  |  |
|  |  |  |
|  |  |  |
|  |  |  |
|  |  |  |
|  |  |  |
|  |  |  |
|  |  |  |
|  |  |  |
|  |  |  |

| SALES GENIUS TRAITS | Day 39 Date: | Day 40 Date: |
|---|---|---|
| 1. Peak sales vision | | |
| 2. Planning | | |
| 3. Persistence | | |
| 4. Learning from mistakes | | |
| 5. Belief in self, company, product/service | | |
| 6. Expertise | | |
| 7. Commitment | | |
| 8. Desire | | |
| 9. Mastermind group | | |
| 10. Truth and honesty | | |
| 11. Imagination | | |
| 12. Energy | | |

| Day 41 | Day 42 | Day 43 |
|--------|--------|--------|
| Date: | Date: | Date: |
|  |  |  |
|  |  |  |
|  |  |  |
|  |  |  |
|  |  |  |
|  |  |  |
|  |  |  |
|  |  |  |
|  |  |  |
|  |  |  |
|  |  |  |
|  |  |  |

| SALES GENIUS TRAITS | Day 44 Date: | Day 45 Date: |
|---|---|---|
| 1.  Peak sales vision | | |
| 2.  Planning | | |
| 3.  Persistence | | |
| 4.  Learning from mistakes | | |
| 5.  Belief in self, company, product/service | | |
| 6.  Expertise | | |
| 7.  Commitment | | |
| 8.  Desire | | |
| 9.  Mastermind group | | |
| 10.  Truth and honesty | | |
| 11.  Imagination | | |
| 12.  Energy | | |

| Day 46 | Day 47 | Day 48 |
|---|---|---|
| Date: | Date: | Date: |
|  |  |  |
|  |  |  |
|  |  |  |
|  |  |  |
|  |  |  |
|  |  |  |
|  |  |  |
|  |  |  |
|  |  |  |
|  |  |  |
|  |  |  |
|  |  |  |

| SALES GENIUS TRAITS | Day 49 | Day 50 |
|---|---|---|
| | Date: | Date: |
| 1.   Peak sales vision | | |
| 2.   Planning | | |
| 3.   Persistence | | |
| 4.   Learning from mistakes | | |
| 5.   Belief in self, company, product/service | | |
| 6.   Expertise | | |
| 7.   Commitment | | |
| 8.   Desire | | |
| 9.   Mastermind group | | |
| 10.   Truth and honesty | | |
| 11.   Imagination | | |
| 12.   Energy | | |

| Day 51 | Day 52 | Day 53 |
|--------|--------|--------|
| Date: | Date: | Date: |
| | | |
| | | |
| | | |
| | | |
| | | |
| | | |
| | | |
| | | |
| | | |
| | | |
| | | |

| SALES GENIUS TRAITS | Day 54 | Day 55 |
|---|---|---|
| | Date: | Date: |
| 1.   Peak sales vision | | |
| 2.   Planning | | |
| 3.   Persistence | | |
| 4.   Learning from mistakes | | |
| 5.   Belief in self, company, product/service | | |
| 6.   Expertise | | |
| 7.   Commitment | | |
| 8.   Desire | | |
| 9.   Mastermind group | | |
| 10.   Truth and honesty | | |
| 11.   Imagination | | |
| 12.   Energy | | |

| Day 56 | Day 57 | Day 58 |
|--------|--------|--------|
| Date: | Date: | Date: |
| | | |
| | | |
| | | |
| | | |
| | | |
| | | |
| | | |
| | | |
| | | |
| | | |
| | | |
| | | |

| SALES GENIUS TRAITS | Day 59 | Day 60 |
|---|---|---|
| | Date: | Date: |
| 1.   Peak sales vision | | |
| 2.   Planning | | |
| 3.   Persistence | | |
| 4.   Learning from mistakes | | |
| 5.   Belief in self, company, product/service | | |
| 6.   Expertise | | |
| 7.   Commitment | | |
| 8.   Desire | | |
| 9.   Mastermind group | | |
| 10.  Truth and honesty | | |
| 11.  Imagination | | |
| 12.  Energy | | |

| Day 61 | Day 62 | Day 63 |
|---|---|---|
| Date: | Date: | Date: |
|  |  |  |
|  |  |  |
|  |  |  |
|  |  |  |
|  |  |  |
|  |  |  |
|  |  |  |
|  |  |  |
|  |  |  |
|  |  |  |
|  |  |  |
|  |  |  |

| SALES GENIUS TRAITS | Day 64 | Day 65 |
|---|---|---|
| | Date: | Date: |
| 1.  Peak sales vision | | |
| 2.  Planning | | |
| 3.  Persistence | | |
| 4.  Learning from mistakes | | |
| 5.  Belief in self, company, product/service | | |
| 6.  Expertise | | |
| 7.  Commitment | | |
| 8.  Desire | | |
| 9.  Mastermind group | | |
| 10.  Truth and honesty | | |
| 11.  Imagination | | |
| 12.  Energy | | |

| Day 66 | Score |
|---|---|
| Date: | |
| | |
| | |
| | |
| | |
| | |
| | |
| | |
| | |
| | |
| | |
| | |
| | |

Place your scores on the Sales Genius Traits
Master Progress Sheet on page 82.

| SALES GENIUS TRAITS | Day 67 Date: | Day 68 Date: |
|---|---|---|
| 1. Peak sales vision | | |
| 2. Planning | | |
| 3. Persistence | | |
| 4. Learning from mistakes | | |
| 5. Belief in self, company, product/service | | |
| 6. Expertise | | |
| 7. Commitment | | |
| 8. Desire | | |
| 9. Mastermind group | | |
| 10. Truth and honesty | | |
| 11. Imagination | | |
| 12. Energy | | |

| Day 69 | Day 70 | Day 71 |
|---|---|---|
| Date: | Date: | Date: |
| | | |
| | | |
| | | |
| | | |
| | | |
| | | |
| | | |
| | | |
| | | |
| | | |
| | | |
| | | |

| SALES GENIUS TRAITS | Day 72 | Day 73 |
|---|---|---|
|  | Date: | Date: |
| 1.  Peak sales vision | | |
| 2.  Planning | | |
| 3.  Persistence | | |
| 4.  Learning from mistakes | | |
| 5.  Belief in self, company, product/service | | |
| 6.  Expertise | | |
| 7.  Commitment | | |
| 8.  Desire | | |
| 9.  Mastermind group | | |
| 10.  Truth and honesty | | |
| 11.  Imagination | | |
| 12.  Energy | | |

| Day 74 | Day 75 | Day 76 |
|---|---|---|
| Date: | Date: | Date: |
|  |  |  |
|  |  |  |
|  |  |  |
|  |  |  |
|  |  |  |
|  |  |  |
|  |  |  |
|  |  |  |
|  |  |  |
|  |  |  |
|  |  |  |
|  |  |  |

| SALES GENIUS TRAITS | Day 77 | Day 78 |
|---|---|---|
| | Date: | Date: |
| 1. Peak sales vision | | |
| 2. Planning | | |
| 3. Persistence | | |
| 4. Learning from mistakes | | |
| 5. Belief in self, company, product/service | | |
| 6. Expertise | | |
| 7. Commitment | | |
| 8. Desire | | |
| 9. Mastermind group | | |
| 10. Truth and honesty | | |
| 11. Imagination | | |
| 12. Energy | | |

| Day 79 | Day 80 | Day 81 |
|--------|--------|--------|
| Date: | Date: | Date: |
| | | |
| | | |
| | | |
| | | |
| | | |
| | | |
| | | |
| | | |
| | | |
| | | |
| | | |
| | | |

| SALES GENIUS TRAITS | Day 82 Date: | Day 83 Date: |
|---|---|---|
| 1.  Peak sales vision | | |
| 2.  Planning | | |
| 3.  Persistence | | |
| 4.  Learning from mistakes | | |
| 5.  Belief in self, company, product/service | | |
| 6.  Expertise | | |
| 7.  Commitment | | |
| 8.  Desire | | |
| 9.  Mastermind group | | |
| 10.  Truth and honesty | | |
| 11.  Imagination | | |
| 12.  Energy | | |

| Day 84 | Day 85 | Day 86 |
|---|---|---|
| Date: | Date: | Date: |
|  |  |  |
|  |  |  |
|  |  |  |
|  |  |  |
|  |  |  |
|  |  |  |
|  |  |  |
|  |  |  |
|  |  |  |
|  |  |  |
|  |  |  |
|  |  |  |

| SALES GENIUS TRAITS | Day 87 | Day 88 |
|---|---|---|
| | Date: | Date: |
| 1.  Peak sales vision | | |
| 2.  Planning | | |
| 3.  Persistence | | |
| 4.  Learning from mistakes | | |
| 5.  Belief in self, company, product/service | | |
| 6.  Expertise | | |
| 7.  Commitment | | |
| 8.  Desire | | |
| 9.  Mastermind group | | |
| 10.  Truth and honesty | | |
| 11.  Imagination | | |
| 12.  Energy | | |

| Day 89 | Day 90 | Day 91 |
|--------|--------|--------|
| Date: | Date: | Date: |
| | | |
| | | |
| | | |
| | | |
| | | |
| | | |
| | | |
| | | |
| | | |
| | | |
| | | |
| | | |

| SALES GENIUS TRAITS | Day 92 | Day 93 |
|---|---|---|
| | Date: | Date: |
| 1.   Peak sales vision | | |
| 2.   Planning | | |
| 3.   Persistence | | |
| 4.   Learning from mistakes | | |
| 5.   Belief in self, company, product/service | | |
| 6.   Expertise | | |
| 7.   Commitment | | |
| 8.   Desire | | |
| 9.   Mastermind group | | |
| 10.   Truth and honesty | | |
| 11.   Imagination | | |
| 12.   Energy | | |

| Day 94 | Day 95 | Day 96 |
|---|---|---|
| Date: | Date: | Date: |
| | | |
| | | |
| | | |
| | | |
| | | |
| | | |
| | | |
| | | |
| | | |
| | | |
| | | |
| | | |

| SALES GENIUS TRAITS | Day 97 | Day 98 |
|---|---|---|
| | Date: | Date: |
| 1.   Peak sales vision | | |
| 2.   Planning | | |
| 3.   Persistence | | |
| 4.   Learning from mistakes | | |
| 5.   Belief in self, company, product/service | | |
| 6.   Expertise | | |
| 7.   Commitment | | |
| 8.   Desire | | |
| 9.   Mastermind group | | |
| 10.  Truth and honesty | | |
| 11.  Imagination | | |
| 12.  Energy | | |

| Day 99 | Day 100 | Score |
|--------|---------|-------|
| Date: | Date: | |
| | | |
| | | |
| | | |
| | | |
| | | |
| | | |
| | | |
| | | |
| | | |
| | | |
| | | |
| | | |

Place your scores on the Sales Genius Traits Master Progress Sheet on page 82.

# Index of activities

## Sensory intelligence

## Intuitive intelligence

## Logical intelligence

# Verbal intelligence

# Spatial intelligence

# Personal intelligence

# Musical intelligence

# Mind–body intelligence

# People intelligence

# Technical intelligence

# Visual intelligence

# Creative intelligence

# Summary of Sales Genius learning points

| The 12 traits of a Sales Genius | The 12 sales intelligences | The 10 cortical skills | The 5 senses and 5 functions |
|---|---|---|---|
| • Peak sales vision | • Sensory | • Numbers | • Sound |
| • Planning | • Intuitive | • Words | • Sight |
| • Persistence | • Logical | • Logic | • Smell |
| • Learning from mistakes | • Verbal | • Lists | • Taste |
| • Belief in self, company, product/service | • Spatial | • Details | • Touch |
| • Expertise | • Personal | • Pictures | • Receiving |
| • Commitment | • Musical | • Imagination | • Holding |
| • Desire | • Mind–body | • Colour | • Analysing |
| • Mastermind group | • People | • Rhythm | • Outputting |
| • Truth and honesty | • Technical | • Space | • Controlling |
| • Imagination | • Visual | | |
| • Energy | • Creative | | |

# Resources

For all information concerning Buzan's Mental Literacy courses, Mind Sports Olympiad, Mind Maps® and products including MindManager software, please contact:

*in North America*
Buzan Centres Inc.
P.O. Box 4
Palm Beach
FL 33480
USA
E-mail: Buzan@Mind-Map.com
Website: www.Mind-Map.com

*in Europe and the rest of the World*
Buzan Centres Ltd
54 Parkstone Road, Poole
Dorset BH15 2PG
England
Tel: 44 (0) 1202 674676
Fax: 44 (0) 1202 674776
E-mail: Buzan@Mind-Map.com
Website: www.Mind-Map.com

For the Conni Gordon Four-Step Method please contact:

Conni Gordon Convention Presentations
427 – 22nd Street
Miami Beach
FL 33139
USA
Tel: 1 (305) 532-1001
Fax: 1 (305) 532-5811
E-mail: connigordn@aol.com

# Index

*Note*: All references are to page numbers. Those in *italics* relate to the activities listed in Part Three.